THE
EVERYDAY
LEADER

Advance Praise

"Every leader, regardless of where they are on their journey, should read this book! We all need a reminder about the real-world application of the Marine Corps leadership traits to business. Their methods have never been more relevant than they are today! *The Everyday Leader* is a fresh and inviting reflection of those traits. A must read!"

—**Chris Dyer**, CEO of PeopleG2, Best-Selling Author and International Speaker

"Upon my retirement from the Marine Corps, I anticipated that I would need to make a significant shift in my leadership style. I was wrong! I found that the Leadership Traits I learned as a Marine were every bit as relevant in the business world as they were in the Corps. *The Everyday Leader* highlights the timeless value of those lessons in a manner that is clear, succinct, articulate and impactful. Sharing their stories and experiences, Hema and Michael have done an outstanding job of demonstrating the incredible power and pertinence of those fourteen leadership traits—to every leader!"

—**Bill Birnie**, President & CEO, Frontwave Credit Union

"These fourteen leadership traits aren't just concepts; these traits are meant to encourage leaders to establish their own leadership traits that convert to actions and actual strategies to lead confidently in the boardroom and in everyday life. I you are a student of leadership you will want to study this book!"

—**Chester Elton**, Best-selling author of *The Carrot Principle* and *Leading with Gratitude*

"The Everyday Leader will inspire anyone anywhere to lead! It grabs your attention through the heroic stories of our U.S. Marine Corps; it provides real and applicable examples of how to lead and teaches you tangible leadership habits you can apply every day. This book will help you evolve into a better leader, plain and simple!"

—**Joe Musselman**, Founder, The Honor Foundation and Fathom VC

"*The Everyday Leader* is a phenomenal study of leadership in the twenty-first century. By describing the Marine Corps leadership traits and relating them to real world events, Hema and Michael have shown that these leadership traits are not only the tools that the Marine Corps use to coach, teach, and mentor; companies can also use these leaderships traits to become successful. *The Everyday Leader* provides an interesting perspective on leadership, mentorship, and how to become successful members of any team."

—**Sergeant Major Jody Armentrout**, (USMC)

"Hema and Michael take a simple, relatable and real-world approach to leadership in this practical guide. As someone who has held leadership positions across several industries, I appreciated *The Everyday Leader* for its breadth of content and wide applicability. As a behavior scientist, I loved the book's focus on valuable behaviors that *anyone* can learn. This is your go-to leadership guide!"

—**Gianna Biscontini**, Executive Coach, Wylde & Well and Co-Founder, Courageous Leadership

"The world is in desperate need of a new type of leader. Servant leadership is woven into the culture of the military. Through stories, *The Everyday Leader* introduces you to this selfless style of leadership and its lasting impact. It takes you on a journey of how to adopt this proven leadership style into your organizational culture and your everyday life."

—**Joe Lara**, VP Programs and Curriculum at
The Honor Foundation

"Michael and Hema have blended their military and leadership experience to create compelling evidence into how to be a better leader. If each of us adopted and applied the principles of *The Everyday Leader*, it would not only create winning outcomes for business, but we could also all change the world!"

—**Stephen Axel**, Principal, Axel Coaching

"Excellent resource that incorporates proven military leadership principles into everyday life. The vignettes thoughtfully reinforce the lessons learned and will improve any organization or individual's leadership abilities. Highly recommend!"

—**Captain P.J. Long** (USMC Retired)

"*The Everyday Leader* combines many valuable lessons from a distinguished career in the Marine Corps. More importantly, Hema and Michael have created something that applies to non-military leaders too. There are many insights from Marine leadership that can inspire and help people in the world of business. I think that this book is an excellent way to help promote better leadership in the corporate world by applying wisdom from the military."

—**Captain Tim Rose** (USMC Reserve), Vice President,
Drexel Hamilton

"Over a career in the Marine Corps I learned to judge the quality of a leader not by what he or she could do; rather, effective leadership can best be seen in the actions and attitudes of men and women who are inspired by their leaders. *The Everyday Leader* is a guide that passes on a lifetime of valuable leadership lessons to professionals of all experience levels. I am thrilled that a single publication captures the importance of our coveted leadership traits and provides relevant examples of how they can be put into action."

—**Captain Michael Davidson**, (USMC)

THE EVERYDAY LEADER

14 MARINE CORPS TRAITS TO UNLOCK YOUR LEADERSHIP DNA

Hema Crockett
Michael Crockett

NEW YORK

LONDON • NASHVILLE • MELBOURNE • VANCOUVER

THE EVERYDAY LEADER
14 Marine Corps Traits to Unlock Your Leadership DNA

Published in New York, New York, by Morgan James Publishing. Morgan James is a trademark of Morgan James, LLC. www.MorganJamesPublishing.com

ISBN 9781631953675 paperback
ISBN 9781631953682 eBook
Library of Congress Control Number: 2020948155

Cover Design by:
Rachel Lopez
www.r2cdesign.com

Interior Design by:
Melissa Farr
melissa@backporchcreative.com

Author Photos by:
Let's Frolic Together

Morgan James is a proud partner of Habitat for Humanity Peninsula and Greater Williamsburg. Partners in building since 2006.

Get involved today! Visit
MorganJamesPublishing.com/giving-back

TABLE OF CONTENTS

ACKNOWLEDGMENTS

Writing a book is a team effort. Writing a book when you're married to the co-author is a test. We never thought we'd write a book together, and it has been an amazing journey and learning experience, and we are grateful for each other. We would also like to thank Mom and Dad, who read every chapter along the way and who provided their insights and comments. It was necessary and hugely appreciated. Thank you to Rea Frey Holguin, who helped guide us long before *The Everyday Leader* was even an idea. We'd also like to thank our business partner and, more importantly, dear friend Jamie Jacobs for her support and encouragement. Thank you to the US Marine Corps for instilling these traits into every leader and for serving as the inspiration for what we wanted to create. Thank you to our friends and colleagues for your unwavering support, contributions to this book, and for the wisdom you have shared over the years. And last but certainly not least, thank you to David Hancock and Morgan James Publishing for taking a chance on us. We are forever grateful.

FOREWORD

I joined the State Department in 1981. I was twenty-eight years old and fleeing the prospect of having to put my law degree to work in the real world. I didn't join to change the world. I didn't join to be a crusader. I joined because I needed a job and the State Department offered me one. The rest, as they say, is history.

When I joined, I never expected to be an Ambassador, much less to have the honor to serve our nation three times as an American Ambassador; first to Eritrea, representing President George W. Bush and then to Nepal and Uganda, as the representative of President Barack Obama. Nor did I anticipate that, along the way, a commitment to service in pursuit of values in which I believed would come to be the defining principle and driving force in my life. But it did. And it remains so today.

Values matter. To me, the values embodied in our founding documents matter. Values that recognize the intrinsic dignity we all share. Values that call upon us to stand for freedom, to speak for those who cannot speak for themselves, and to fight against oppression – whether from dictators or the oppression of grinding poverty. Those values served to inform the leader I became and, knowing what I believed in and why I served, was critical to my achieving whatever measure of success I experienced in service to our nation.

And that is perhaps why *The Everyday Leader* resonates so strongly for me. Hema and Michael know that leadership is about values and about vision. They understand that leadership isn't something we "practice" from nine to five. We don't put it on and take it off at the end of the day like our workplace wardrobe. They remind us that leadership isn't about titles or rank. It is intrinsic to who we are.

Hema and Michael draw upon the defining values that were part of Michael's service in the Marine Corps to shape their discussion of leadership, and I can understand why. These were values that Michael internalized as part of his service and I saw him display them again and again when he led our Marine Security Guard Detachment in Nepal. And I saw those same values reflected in all the Marines with whom I worked over the years – from four-star generals to a young corporal in a Marine Security Guard detachment. Although our institutional cultures might have been very different, I came to realize that the values that define leadership in the Corps were universal.

These are the values that Michael and Hema talk about. They emphasize the critical importance of integrity and moral courage. They know that vision and strength of character are essential. And they remind us that leadership isn't about us – it's about those who trust us to lead them.

And, underlying every part of their narrative, is the compelling reminder that, even as we demand the best from ourselves and our teams, we must never forget that our humanity, decency and empathy are every bit as important as our ability to be clear, decisive and directive.

Michael and Hema know all this. They have practiced it in the Corps and in the business world, respectively. They know that good leaders don't succeed because they have the authority to impose his or her will. They succeed because they have the vision to guide their team towards a goal grounded in shared values.

Leadership isn't about wielding power. It is about accepting responsibility. It is about respecting the team that supports you. It is about giving them the leadership that they deserve.

Loyalty, honor, dignity, integrity. That's true leadership. That's what *The Everyday Leader* is all about and that's why I'm so proud to have had this chance to applaud what Hema and Michael have crafted.

Semper Fi.

Ambassador (ret) Scott DeLisi
U.S. State Department
Author of *The Ambassador's Dog*

CHAPTER 1

JUDGMENT

*The ability to weigh facts and possible courses of action
in order to make sound decisions.*

Complacency Kills. This is what was painted on the barriers before leaving the Forward Operating Base in Fallujah. I saw this sign every day for months. (This was also what I had preached to my Marines.)

The day before leaving Iraq, it was over one hundred degrees before 6:00 a.m. As soon as I woke up, I could detect the strong sulfur smell from the previous night's gunfights mixed with burning debris. I started my day by shaving, brushing my teeth, and eating my morning MRE (Meal Ready to Eat). After checking in at the command center and attending my various morning meetings, I went to check on my Marines at the security posts.

After checking in on all but one of the security posts, I stopped to pick up a couple of MREs for my Marines before walking to my last post. MREs tucked safely in my pockets, I began the walk out of the soda factory and over to the back building, the one with the great panoramic field of vision. I had on all of my combat gear, with my rifle and helmet in hand. I began walking up the steps of the back building to go outside on the deck. As soon as my head became visible over the three-foot-high wall, the distinct *snap-hiss* of a bullet whizzed by the right side of my head. The bullet was close enough for me to feel the unmistakable movement of air on my head and ears as it went by.

In that moment, walking up those steps, I was complacent. I knew that I should have been wearing my helmet and keeping my head down. It was something I reiterated to the Marines ad nauseam. Up until the moment the bullet rocketed past my head, my mind was a million miles away.

As I put the helmet on and fastened the chin strap, I looked over at my Marines. The look of sheer terror in their eyes told me there was a sniper on a distant rooftop. I grabbed a radio to report the sniper fire back to the base, and I heard the friendly sound of a helicopter and then two rockets impacting their targets. The explosion was in the same general location where the sniper shot had come from. A few minutes later, confirmation came through on the radio that the insurgent sniper would no longer be a threat. I was truly lucky to be alive.

In the business world, while we don't have literal bullets flying at our heads like I did in Fallujah, we are bombarded with things to do and decisions that need to be made on a daily basis. In order to be effective at our jobs and stay alive, so to speak, we need to have a high level of judgment and the ability to make good decisions.

So, what is judgment anyway? The Marine Corps identifies and describes its fourteen leadership traits in Marine Corps Reference Publication 6-11B. They define judgment as "the ability to weigh facts and possible courses of action in order to make sound decisions." The business community would use the same definition.

Experience would tell us that judgment is a key ingredient in leadership. We need to be able to come to sensible conclusions with the information that we have. But why is judgment so hard when we're actually put into business situations that require high levels of it? Oftentimes, it's fear. We're scared of the consequences if we make the wrong decision, and we second-guess ourselves. Other times we think we're making the right decision when, in fact, we are not. Or, as in my situation, our heads are not in the game, and we're making decisions without thinking clearly.

A number of years back, Hema worked for a start-up company. She was speaking with a manager who was worried that one of his employees was suicidal. He found a knife on this employee's desk, and rather than calling HR or even his own manager, he proceeded to pick up the knife and take it home with him. Hema couldn't figure out why the manager would do such a thing, so she asked him. His response was, "Because I wanted to get the knife away from the employee as quickly as possible." He made the best decision he could with the information he had, based on his own experience. He weighed his options—it was late, and Hema might have gone home, and he didn't want the employee to hurt himself. How many of us would have made the same decision in the moment? It's hard to say unless we're in the situation.

What Makes Good Judgment?

We know judgment is important in our personal and professional lives, but what makes good judgment? What are the elements that need to come together to ensure we are making the best and most sound decisions in the absence of clear-cut evidence? It starts with knowledge and understanding. It's not enough to *know* something.

You need to be able to understand it and give it meaning…and you can't jump to a decision. Understanding information is about being able to critically think about what you're reading and hearing. Furthermore, it's about putting aside our own filters and biases so we obtain a full picture of the information and don't just hear what we want to hear.

Think back to a performance review in your career that stands out. Maybe it was early on. Why does this particular review stand out for you? Perhaps it was because it was the first time you were provided negative feedback or given an area of improvement. Many managers provide feedback using the sandwich method—sandwiching potentially negative feedback between two positive comments.

Thinking back on your review, did your manager do this, and are you choosing to filter out the positive because you are focusing on the negative? The ability to understand and think critically is about listening to *all* of the information and absorbing *all* of the information in order to make a sound decision and not basing a decision off of what we choose to hear. In your review, what was the tone of your manager? What was their body language? Good judgment is deeper than what someone is saying. It's about what they're not saying.

Body language tells us a lot about a situation. Remember, this interpretation goes both ways. As much as you are reading other people's body language, they are reading yours. Are your arms crossed? Are you rolling your eyes or sighing when someone is speaking? While awareness of body language is critical for everyone, it's even more important for leaders. People are looking to you for guidance and direction. Is there alignment between what you're saying verbally and what your body language and tone are saying?

Another characteristic that helps leaders practice good judgment is seeking diverse and differing opinions. Wouldn't it be amazing if everyone just agreed with us and validated our ideas and solutions? While we'd like to think this would be amazing, our ideas aren't always the only…or the right…ones. We know, we know. It took us years to figure this one out ourselves. We need diversity of thought and experiences to help us come to the best decisions. This comes from asking others their thoughts and opinions and truly listening to what they are saying.

A quick note on listening. There are three levels of listening. In level one listening, the focus is on you. You're not really listening to what the other person is saying, you are just preparing to respond. Your focus is on what you're going to say. Not much listening is really happening here. Level two listening is focused on the other person. You are listening to what they are saying, are nodding your head in agreement or in acknowledgement. The other person feels heard. You are listening with curiosity because you are genuinely interested in what the other person has to say. You may even ask some questions. Level three listening is about the collective: you and the other person and the energy that is created during your conversation. You are listening to words, but you are also sensing body language, tone, and feeling. You are in the present, engaged and asking questions as appropriate. Level three listening is often the hardest for most of us yet is also the most valuable. Try to be between a level two and level three when asking others for their opinions and viewpoints so you can make a sound decision.

Asking for opinions and opposing viewpoints shouldn't be intimidating and shouldn't make you feel as if you aren't qualified to make a decision. On the contrary, it actually shows your self-awareness and ability to understand your strengths and tap into the strengths of others (another quality of strong leaders). If you did a side-by-side comparison of Mark Zuckerberg's (CEO of Facebook) resume with that of Sheryl Sandberg's (COO of Facebook), you would see Sandberg's experience far outweighs Zuckerberg's. Yet Zuckerberg sought out and hired Sandberg. Why? Because he saw an opportunity to work with and learn from someone who was smarter than he was when it came to running what was, at the time, a multi-million-dollar organization. Rather than being intimidated by Sandberg, he saw her strengths and her capacity not only to help the organization but also to help him become a better leader. We see this occur throughout business. Jack Ma, co-founder of multinational technology conglomerate Alibaba, hired John Wu of Yahoo to be his Chief Technology Officer. Ma knew his strengths and hired Wu to help him fill a void. There are countless other examples. The point is simple: good judgment requires you to put your ego aside and be open to diverse viewpoints and experiences.

One way to solicit diverse viewpoints is by forming a small group of trusted advisors, people who will keep it real with you and tell you the truth versus what you want to hear. Then lean on this group when making decisions. Use them as a sounding board. As you develop this muscle, you will become more comfortable with routinely asking others for their thoughts. As a leader, engaging your team is key, and this happens by listening to what they are saying.

Another element of good judgment is experience. Draw on your experience to help you make decisions. There's an aphorism we find especially helpful here: "Good judgment is the result of experience and experience the result of bad judgment." (This quote has been attributed to Mark Twain, Oscar Wilde, and Mulla Nasrudin, among others.) While its origin may be unknown, the sentiment is clear: our experience tends to be the number one source of information we use to make decisions. Think about times throughout your career, or perhaps even in your personal life, the ways you handled situations, the conclusions you came to, and the outcomes of those decisions. If you encountered something similar previously and your solution didn't work, how can you adjust it when you see the situation again? What would you do differently?

If you're early in your career, you can expand your experience and gain exposure to many different areas of business. Next time there is a big project, ask to be part of the project team. Not only is this beneficial from an experience perspective, but it also gives you a front-row seat to how others make decisions.

Finally, have awareness. This comes in the form of self-awareness, as we touched upon earlier. Know your strengths and areas where you can use the help of someone else. Also, be aware of your surroundings and the potential unintended consequences of your decisions. Clearly, Mike was not paying enough attention to his surroundings when he decided to walk outside without a helmet on. The unintended consequences of that decision could have been severe—Mike could have lost his life. But the unintended consequence of his Marines seeing him have such a lapse in judgment could also have been detrimental. They could have lost trust in Mike and in his leadership and in his ability to effectively make decisions that kept everyone safe. Think about the consequences your decisions can have.

Marine versus Bicycle

    I was walking into my office at the embassy in Berlin, and I stopped in to say good morning to my boss. He looked up from his computer and asked me to sit down. I was a bit apprehensive, but I thought maybe he just wanted to catch up on a few items. With an odd smile on his face, he said, "You're never going to believe this, but your new Marine crushed a bicycle this morning." Completely confused by what I'd just heard, I asked him to explain. With only minimal information, which was all he knew, he told me that one of his employees had witnessed a bicycle being destroyed by a Marine. It was my job to get the whole story.

    I looked at my schedule to see which Marine was working during the timeframe when the incident took place. I already had a gut feeling about which Marine it was when I met with my boss, but I needed confirmation. I was right; it was my newest Marine, the one who had just graduated Marine Security Guard school. I tracked down the young Marine to ask what happened. Initially, he attempted to be coy about the situation, which resulted in my becoming much more direct in tone and with my questions. Seeing that he was caught, and with no way out, he came clean. The young Marine explained that it was 2:30 a.m., and he had completed his security checks for the evening. With his work 'done,' he was bored. When he looked at the security monitors, he noticed a bicycle leaning against one of the security bollards that surround the embassy building. These bollards are made of solid steel and are designed to keep unauthorized vehicles off of the property. They can be lowered when allowing vehicles to pass. This Marine thought it would be funny to lower the security bollard the bicycle was leaning on, causing the bicycle to fall over. It never occurred to the Marine that the bollard might destroy the bicycle or that he might damage the bollard. At that point, I had heard enough. I told him that because of his lack of judgment, he could no longer be trusted to serve in any security capacity at the embassy. I finished by informing him that I would be requesting that he be sent home. Before I left, I asked the Marine if the laugh was worth a demotion in rank and removal from the Marine Security program. His response was a tear-filled no.

In addition to being reduced in rank by one pay grade and forfeiting a portion of his pay, he would also have to pay over 1,000 Euros to the owner of the bicycle. A few months later, I heard from my successor that this same Marine had another lapse in judgment that resulted in his termination from the program.

In this same vein, question solutions offered by others that you are asked to weigh in on. What are all of the options to choose from? Are you sure these are the only options? Why are people confident that their solution is the best? Also question what execution will look like. An idea can sound wonderful, but if it can't be implemented or if it creates more issues during implementation, then it probably isn't worth it.

It's not a coincidence that we are starting with judgment as we talk about leadership. Strong leadership is predicated on good judgment. Decisions need to be well informed and timely. As you'll see throughout the next chapters as well, leadership isn't about who or how many people you manage. It's about your decision-making, your character and your values.

Putting it into Practice

The good news is, there are many things you can do to improve your decision-making quality and ability. The more you practice each of these, the better you will become.

Write things down. Many of us make a pro/con list when making decisions in our personal lives. The pros/cons of moving to another state. The pros/cons of moving to a certain neighborhood. Even the pros/cons of changing jobs. This same method works when weighing business decisions. And when we write down the options and weigh the pros and cons of each in writing, we tend to think more critically about each one.

Recognize your default bias. We are all strong-wired to make decisions based on our emotions, feelings, and unconscious motives. Notice we didn't say hard-wired. Hard wiring implies we can't change, when we absolutely can. Consider decisions you have made in the past where you've exercised both good and not-so-good judgment. What led you to make the decisions that you did? Are you more intuitive or data-driven when making decisions? How willing are you to take risks? Now, do you see a pattern in your judgment and decision-making? Once you are aware of your default biases, come up with ways to counterbalance them. For example, if you are more intuitive, ask for data before making a decision. If you tend to be risk-averse, consider how much risk is acceptable to you. This awareness will also allow you to be more agile when making decisions, and agility is key to leadership, as organizations are dynamic.

Do you focus on the forest or the trees? There's a saying that goes, "You can't see the forest for the trees." This implies that you are so focused on the details that you lose sight of the big picture, which can narrow your decision-making and can often lead to poor judgment. The opposite problem is also very real, where you focus on the big picture but miss the finer details and points. The goal is to find a balance. You may naturally focus on the forest. That's okay, but before you make a decision, loop back around and ask questions to dig a bit deeper into the details. What would be the first step we take if we choose option A? And if you tend to focus on the trees, consider asking big picture questions: what is the broader impact of the decision I am making?

Good judgment is the foundation of any great leader. As you consider what your personal—as well as organizational—leadership traits are, we would strongly urge you to make judgment one of them.

CHAPTER 2

JUSTICE

Giving reward and punishment according to
the merits of the case in question.

There was a senior Marine standing at the desk, taking our check-in paperwork before we entered the classroom for the basic machine-gun course. As I handed my paperwork over, I saw the Marine's name on his uniform. It looked familiar, but I couldn't place it. He recognized my name as soon as he saw it on my paperwork, and like in a movie, we looked each other in the eyes at the same time. The memory came rushing back when I recognized his face, and then I could feel my heart start to beat out of my chest.

Two days prior, the same senior Marine had come to my office at 2nd Battalion, 5th Marines because he had not received a paycheck. Rightfully so, he was irritated and his mood only worsened when he saw that I was the only person in the office. It was lunchtime, and I was a private first class, the lowest on the totem pole, with absolutely zero authority. I looked up his pay information in our computer system to diagnose what caused the issue and quickly found it. I nervously informed him that an audit had been completed, and it was discovered that he had been overpaid for the previous six months. He needed to pay back the overpayment, which resulted in his not receiving a paycheck. In addition, he wouldn't receive a paycheck until the government was paid back in full. Upon hearing this, he exploded in a curse-laden rant and stormed off before I could tell him that I could help fix the situation and get him paid.

Now, standing in front of the same senior Marine once again, he angrily told me to stand off to the side and that he would deal with me in a minute. Then he continued to check in the remaining students, allowing them into the classroom.

At 7:31 a.m., he walked over to me with an evil smirk on his face. He told me that I reported late to class and that I would not be allowed to attend the course. He went on to say that he would be notifying my boss that I failed to report to class on time. At that moment, I completely stopped listening to anything he was saying. It wasn't because I couldn't hear him since he was certainly loud enough. I just couldn't stop thinking how unfair this was.

The Marine I drove with arrived at the exact same time as I did, and he was allowed to stay. In fact, there were at least five other Marines who showed up after I did, and they all were allowed in. Forget all of that, we'd arrived at 7:15 a.m., making us early. In that moment, none of that mattered. It was his word against mine. I was four ranks below him. I knew no matter what I said, I would be punished.

A short time later, I arrived back at 2nd Battalion, 5th Marines, where my supervisor was eagerly waiting. He was the command representative the senior Marine had spoken to about my being late. The look in his eyes told me that I would not have a chance to explain what happened. We had a one-way conversation in which my supervisor told me how I'd embarrassed him and the rest of my department and that he was going to make an example out of me. The punishment I received would delay my promotion to the next rank for nine months.

About a year later, I attended and completed the machine-gun course. Luckily for me, the same senior Marine was no longer there. He had been caught selling military gear and was now facing jail time. The day I was kicked out of class taught me a lesson that I tried to apply in any situation when dealing with others. The lesson was to listen before reacting, ask questions, and try to understand the intent. This allowed me to gather the facts, and more importantly, allowed everyone to be treated fairly and feel that they had been heard.

Sometimes when we hear the word "justice," visions of lawyers, judges, vindication, revenge, or even comic books may come to mind. Justice isn't relegated to only those who practice law. Justice is an important part of being a leader, especially when leading a team. Clearly, in my situation, justice was not served. Vindication and revenge were.

The Marine Corps defines justice as, "Giving reward and punishment according to the merits of the case in question. The ability to administer a system of rewards and punishments impartially and consistently." If you Googled "justice," you would find a few definitions, most pertaining to righteousness, fairness, equitability, and moral rightness. While the Marine Corps may look at justice from a reward and punishment perspective, the business world tends to look at justice from the perspective of fairness and moral and ethical values. Yes, rewards and punishments play into that. But, for the business world, it's less about the actual reward or punishment and more about whether these are necessary and administered fairly.

What is Organizational Justice?

Believe it or not, organizational justice is a real concept within companies. While we don't necessarily talk about it in these terms, the foundation of any organizational culture is built upon the concepts of trust and integrity. As employees, if we don't believe the internal system of justice works within our organization, then we can't have trust in our organization to do the right thing. This is true of leaders as well. If employees don't perceive their leaders treat everyone fairly and equitably, then there is no foundation of trust and the perception of the leader is tarnished. Notice that we said "perception." Perception is reality, and this is important for all leaders to remember. For example, if there is a perception that some employees are allowed to get away with bad behavior without repercussions, employees will build a story that this particular employee receives preferential treatment or that the leader is incapable of leading. More on this in a minute.

Your Role as Leader

Organizational justice doesn't exist without leaders. The role of a leader in administering justice is extremely important and relies on a few different principles.

First, as a leader, it is your responsibility to ensure equal discipline for equal offenses. If we're talking about fairness, this is the number one place where the concepts of justice and trust can derail a leader's effectiveness. What happened to Mike in his class wasn't fair. He showed up on time, early in fact, and was still kicked out for something he didn't actually do. Others who arrived after he did were allowed to stay. There's one punishment. Then, when talking with his boss, he wasn't even given an opportunity to explain the situation and was instead made an example of. There's the second punishment. This is unfair and unequal discipline. Think back throughout your career or even your childhood. Did you ever say, "That's not fair"? Chances are, you did. We all did at some point. Why did you say it? Was there unequal treatment occurring where perhaps one person was being rewarded or punished more than others in the same circumstance? That was an example of injustice in an organizational context.

In one of the organizations Hema worked for years ago, during the monthly all-hands department meetings, the head of the department would call out employees for their extraordinary work on a recent project or trial (this was a biotech company). However, even though the projects or trials were group based, meaning it took more than one employee to complete them, usually only two to three employees were recognized for their work. Funnily enough, it was usually the same two to three employees month after month. When annual performance review time came around, these same employees were the star performers. The other employees lost trust in their department leader and didn't believe that he looked at performance fairly. While they still completed their projects and trials, these employees stopped giving 100% effort to their jobs. Sound familiar? We're sure you've seen something like this throughout your career as well.

As a leader, it is critical that you are consistent. This doesn't just apply to those leaders who manage people. As we've said before, you don't need to manage people to be a leader. As it relates to justice, all leaders should treat everyone fairly.

You Can Have Your Ice Cream and Eat it Too

We had completed the first month of boot camp the week before Christmas. It was a wet Friday evening, and my platoon was lined up in front of the mess hall, waiting to enter. We were still early in our training, and the focus was on discipline and following orders. Our drill instructor was not-so-subtly reminding us that we were still not Marines, but recruits, and therefore we could not look at, let alone eat, dessert. All ninety-eight recruits acknowledged the order in unison with a loud "Yes, sir," and then, one by one, we entered the mess hall.

I went through the line, got my food and drink, and sat down. With my head down, like we normally ate and were told to eat, I began devouring my dinner. We were not allowed to talk to each other or even look up from our tray. To get caught by a drill instructor doing any of these things meant public embarrassment and certain punishment. As I finished my meal, out of the corner of my eye I noticed another recruit from my platoon get up…unprompted. Simultaneously, I was intrigued by what he was doing and scared for what might follow. I continued to track him without lifting my head. He walked directly over to the ice cream machine, served himself some soft-serve vanilla ice cream, and walked back to his seat. I prayed that I was the only one who had seen this. We finished eating, and the squad leaders led my platoon back outside. At that point, I thought no one else had seen the ice-cream incident, and we were in the clear. In short order, I would find out how wrong I was.

We marched back to our squad bay where we slept. There, the drill instructor was pacing up and down the long opening between our rows of bunks, glaring at each recruit as we stood in front of our steel bunk beds. It was then that I knew I wasn't the only one who saw the ice cream eating. The drill instructor erupted in a loud and vicious tirade for the next thirty minutes, which left us no doubt that we all were in trouble because one recruit defied his orders.

Thirty minutes seems oddly specific. Well, there was a requirement that drill instructors couldn't require any sort of physical exertion for thirty minutes after eating. His rant went on just long enough for our food to settle in our stomachs. I knew what was coming next. We were either going to have to hold flip-flops out in front of us for fifteen minutes without lowering our arms. Or we were going to have to move all of our mattresses into the bathroom. It doesn't sound so bad, but ninety-eight recruits frantically running with twin-size mattresses into a small bathroom is no easy feat. Or, worst of all, we would have to ride the Harley—squat with our arms in front of us and make vroom-vroom sounds as if we were riding Harleys. I had just eaten, and that was the last thing I wanted to do.

Then the strangest thing happened. The drill instructor yelled for the squad leaders to run up and join him in the front of the room. He slyly asked for the recruit who ate the ice cream to join him as well. The drill instructor had the recruit sit down directly in front of the squad leaders. He was getting a front row seat as the drill instructor began screaming at the squad leaders while having them perform a myriad of exercises.

The recruit who ate the ice cream looked at each squad leader, trying to apologize with his eyes. The remaining ninety-three recruits, myself included, stared at what was happening while trying not to get caught and punished ourselves. Once the squad leaders were completely soaked with sweat, the drill instructor directed them to get back to their positions in front of their bunk beds, where the rest of us were standing. I was confused as to why only the squad leaders were punished and why the recruit who actually ate the ice cream was not. The squad leaders, like the rest of us, could not speak while eating, so they would have been unable to tell the recruit to not get the ice cream and to sit back down.

While the point of boot camp is to get us thinking and acting like one unit, and the job of the squad leader is to ensure we do just this, especially in the absence of the drill instructor, the unfairness of the punishment stays with me to this day. It was inconsistent when we all were punished or when only the squad leaders were punished. There was no rhyme or reason to the randomness. The recruit knew he wasn't allowed to eat the ice cream and did it anyway. He even knew that eating the ice cream could result in everyone being punished, but that didn't stop him. He ate the ice cream and watched others get punished for his actions. In this case, justice was not served; the squad leaders were in a no-win scenario. They were going to be punished whether they stopped the recruit from eating ice cream or not.

In addition to equal discipline, you need to provide prompt resolution to issues that arise. This is especially true for those who do manage others. When employees voice concerns, they should be addressed quickly. "Justice delayed is justice denied" is an old legal principle. It rings true in business as well. The longer you wait to resolve issues, the more you erode any trust you may have built up with employees. Plus, if others notice that you haven't taken action against a complaint, chances are employees will stop voicing concerns and bringing issues up.

When resolving issues and concerns, communicate! Be sure to close the loop with employees or your peers. Timely communication is important to the perception that justice has been served.

Finally, having the right lens is important. If you manage people, step out of your leadership role and put yourself in their shoes. How would they perceive the situation and your decision-making? Are all voices heard equally? Are the organization's policies fair and in alignment with stated values? Are opportunities for advancement equal across the organization? Then think about the intended and unintended consequences of these things.

At a financial firm Hema worked for, the organization created robust maternity and paternity policies, paying new moms and dads for up to sixteen weeks to stay home and bond with their new little ones. It was a very generous policy, and many employees were thrilled to be able to spend extra time with their families without worrying about the financial burden time away can cause. But there were employees who were at different stages in their lives. They were taking care of sick family members or dealing with their own health concerns, causing them to miss work and resulting in financial hardships. The robust maternity and paternity policy felt unequal to these employees. The perception of the new policy was that leadership favored new parents more. This certainly wasn't the intent, but remember perception is reality. In reviewing the new policy, it was determined to be unfair. It was amended and the organization paid up to twelve weeks for all employees who needed to take a leave of absence, whether to care for a new baby, care for a sick family member, or to care for themselves. When seen through the lens of a new parent, the robust maternity and paternity policy was fantastic! They were thrilled to have the time away and not worry about money. For those who weren't in the same situation but missed work due to other health reasons, the policy was unjust. Do you see how lenses matter?

A Note of Caution

We would be remiss if we didn't provide a word of caution as it relates to the leader's role in justice. Believe it or not, a leader can be perceived as too fair or too values driven, occasionally leading them to be looked over for promotion. While it may not make sense on the surface, think about it as an outside observer. Part of a leader's job, especially when managing people, is to make tough decisions when necessary. If the leader is too focused on fairness, they can give too many chances. Think about a poor performer. If the leader continues to explain away the poor performance and give the employee multiple chances without consequences, then what message is the leader really sending? And how will others perceive that? Employees won't think, "Look how fair and just the leader is being in giving the poor performer chance after chance." Instead, they're probably going to think, "I work harder than that poor performer, yet he is still here getting paid. I guess performance really doesn't matter to my leader." The inability to make tough decisions due to wanting to be fair and just at all times can be detrimental to how a leader is seen. Strike a balance between doing the right thing and making the tough calls when necessary.

Putting It into Practice

Being a fair or just leader can be difficult. But, if you can achieve the balance of being fair and being decisive, you will be successful. There are a few things you can start doing today to help you.

Seek to understand. Before jumping to conclusions or making any decisions, seek to understand the situation from multiple angles. To do this, ask open-ended questions versus yes-or-no questions. This applies to leaders who are making the decisions as well as leaders who may perceive a situation as unfair. The more you understand about the situation, the fairer it can seem.

Remember your values. When we perceive a situation as unfair, we can often start lashing out and wanting revenge. Rather than being vindictive, remember your values. Have self-discipline and make decisions and statements with integrity. While it's difficult not to bring our emotions to work, it's important that leaders realize making decisions or handling unfairness needs to be free of emotions.

Know when to throw in the towel. It can be hard to give up. But sometimes it becomes necessary. If you've tried to understand the decision-making within your organization and you still perceive it as unfair (and have numerous examples to back up your statement), it may be time to move on. This can lead to a values misalignment and disengagement. Your performance can and will suffer as well. It's important to remember your worth as a leader.

Remember, while justice isn't necessarily a word we hear at work, it takes the form of fairness and equitability. These are extremely important not to only our organizational cultures, but also to our brand as leaders.

CHAPTER 3

DEPENDABILITY

The certainty of proper performance of duty.

A loud, constant beep was coming from inside our house. The earthquake sensors were going off, louder and longer than we had heard before. It was a Friday evening in September 2011, and we were living in Kathmandu, Nepal. I was on special assignment with the Marine Corps, working with the State Department. The house was shaking side to side, and as Hema and I stood in the kitchen watching a large crack appear in the wall and windows shatter, all I could think was that I knew this day would come—I just didn't know when.

But, I was prepared. I had trained extensively for this, as had my Marines, who guarded the US Embassy, which was located just a few minutes from our house. At least I knew they were safe. The embassy building was a state-of-the-art fortress designed to withstand gunfire, small explosives, and natural disasters. Once the shaking finally stopped, Hema and I ran for the embassy. It was my responsibility to ensure our emergency safety procedures for all diplomats in Kathmandu were activated, and I wasn't about to leave Hema behind.

Within minutes, we were at the embassy. Once on the compound, I made my way to the operations center. This command center was manned by a Marine twenty-four hours a day, seven days a week. My second-in-command was already there and was moving into action. While we hadn't experienced an earthquake of this magnitude in Kathmandu before, we were well versed in the embassy's in-depth emergency plan. We knew the structurally weak points within the building, the equipment and systems that needed to be turned off in case of a natural disaster, and all the entrances and exits on and off the embassy compound, in the event chaos ensued. We even ran drills, or practices, timing ourselves to see how quickly we could go through the earthquake plan and address any gaps early, before an actual natural disaster struck. Much like an earthquake, these drills were unplanned and spontaneous, occurring at any hour of the day or night. The Marines were prepared. I knew I could rely on them when the earthquake occurred, and most importantly, the US Ambassador and the State Department knew they could count on us to ensure the other diplomats were safe as well.

All of the Marines were accounted for and were going through their assigned procedures. Each knew what they were responsible for, and each was responding quickly. Then came the part of the plan over which I had limited control, attempting to gain accountability for every State Department employee at the embassy. Each employee had a unique call sign assigned to them, and every weekend, the Marines would perform a radio check, where each employee, using radio etiquette, was responsible for responding with their particular call sign over the radio. These radio call-ins were important because this was the exact procedure each employee or family member would have to follow in the event of an earthquake.

I asked Hema and my second-in-command to initiate the radio callbacks for the embassy employees. While Hema hadn't trained with us, I knew I could count on her to help. After about four hours of radio calls, all 150 employees and their families were accounted for. The embassy building didn't sustain any damage, and the compound remained secured.

The after action report that I would draft for the embassy would highlight the reliable performance of all involved, Marines and non-Marines alike. The continuous training had developed a muscle memory that allowed everyone to know exactly what was required of them and when. I'll always remember checking on my Marines as the radio calls were being made. I wanted to ensure they were okay. Not only were they fine, they were focused and doing exactly as we had trained. In that moment, I knew that no matter the crisis, this was a group of Marines I could depend on. They were the epitome of how the Marine Corps defines dependability, "The certainty of proper performance of duty."

In the business world, we wouldn't necessarily use the same phrasing, but we would define dependability in much the same way. A leader is dependable when we can rely on them to do their job with integrity and be accountable for their actions. We all know people in our personal lives who are dependable. They are the ones we can count on when we have a problem or need advice. Now think about a dependable person you work with or have worked with in the past. What characteristics did they have that made them dependable? Perhaps they were reliable or trustworthy. Perhaps they were accountable and didn't make excuses. Was the person you were thinking of your boss? For most of us, the answer is no. The first person that comes to mind is a peer, a friend at work. Rarely is the person our manager. Why is that? If dependability is such an important leadership trait, shouldn't we expect our manager to be dependable? The answer is yes, and it's further proof that you don't need to manage people to be a leader. Seeing a theme yet?

Elements of Dependability

In short, we place a lot of importance on people and businesses that consistently deliver great results and that follow through on their commitments and promises. And rightfully so. We expect so many services in our lives to be dependable—the internet/cable company, the electric company, the airlines, the car dealerships who service our cars…the list goes on and on. We should expect that the people we work with, and definitely those in leadership positions, are dependable too.

There are quite a few elements to dependability. These characteristics singularly don't make someone dependable. Rather, collectively they must all exist in order for a leader to be viewed as dependable by others.

Do what you say you're going to do. Then do more. Perhaps the most basic, yet most important, element of dependability is keeping your word. If you say you'll be at the office by 8:00 a.m., be there by 8:00 a.m. Better yet, be there by 7:50 a.m. If you say you're going to finish the project by 5:00 p.m., have it completed by 5:00 p.m. or earlier. If you set a meeting to talk with one of your employees, keep the meeting! As a leader, the worst thing you can do is to say that you're going to do something and then not do it! At its core, dependability is about trust (someone else being worthy of your trust, and you being worthy of someone else's trust). If you don't follow through, that trust is eroded.

One place where this element of dependability is seen is during one-on-one meetings between employees and their managers. Hema worked for an organization years ago where one-on-ones were one of the main touchpoints between employees and their managers. Employees would prepare an agenda and be prepared to discuss progress made on various projects, obstacles they were facing when trying to complete a task or project, requests for additional training and developmental opportunities, etc.

Managers would be prepared to discuss whatever the employee wanted to, coach their employees, and provide guidance on how to continue achieving their goals. Managers knew the importance of the one-on-ones, and they had them with their own managers as well. One manager in the IT department would routinely cancel the one-on-ones with their employees. Sometimes, an unexpected emergency situation would arise, which was understandable. Other times, the manager was simply too busy. Worst of all, the manager would cancel these meetings a half hour or less before they were set to occur. These were standing meetings and were on the employee's and manager's calendars. When the meetings would occur, the manager would remind his employees, who had direct reports of their own, the importance of keeping the one-on-ones. What message do you think the manager was sending to the employee? And, if you were those employees, how would you feel? You most certainly wouldn't consider your manager dependable or someone whose word you could trust.

Regardless of your position within the organization, consistently following through on things you say you're going to do is tantamount. However, this is even more so true when you manage others. Put yourself in their shoes and ask yourself, "How would this make me feel?" before you cancel a commitment or fail to follow through. Think about what your actions are saying. For that IT manager, his message was loud and clear: I have better things to do, and you are not a priority.

Be consistent in your actions and results. Most of us have a restaurant or two that we frequent more than others. In fact, we go so often that we know the menu by heart and often order the same meal time and again. The quality of the meal is great. It tastes delicious. And we keep ordering it because we know we can rely on it being amazing. But, have you ever recommended that same meal to a friend, you both order it, and what you receive is different? Your meal came with pasta, like normal, and theirs came with mashed potatoes instead. The next time you go back to that restaurant, you order the same meal, and now you get mashed potatoes. You're a bit confused and have no idea whether you'll get mashed potatoes or pasta the next time you order. Eventually, you get tired and find a new meal altogether. A leader lacking consistency is a bit like that meal—you never know what you're going to get day to day and you don't know what to expect. Could you imagine what would have happened if Mike or his Marines were inconsistent during the earthquake? If they were unable to deliver in that moment of crisis? We don't even want to think about the results.

When a peer or manager comes to you with a question or needing assistance, they are doing so with the assumption that your advice and guidance will be of high quality and in line with advice and guidance you have provided in the past. The same is true for when you are tapped on the shoulder for a new project. Others know they can count on you to not only meet a deadline, but to provide an outstanding work product while asking necessary questions along the way.

When leaders are inconsistent, employees don't know how to act, so they wait. They have to see what they'll be asked to do before taking any action. Even if the employees know what they should do, they will hesitate. This inconsistency caused by the leader will inevitably cause delays and potentially increase costs, not to mention the waste in time and energy. Inconsistency certainly doesn't empower others to take action and think on their own.

Maintain clear and open communication. Finally, communication is key! Dependability doesn't mean you can't change your mind or change a course of action. But, when you do these things, communicate *why* you did them. In general, people don't mind if there is a change in course or a shift in direction; they just want to understand why the change occurred so they don't feel like they wasted their time before.

As a leader, if you are dependable, it is easier for you to require the same of others. This is where clear communication comes in. You expect the project deadline to be met. You expect others to voice concerns or bring up questions if they have them. You expect others to do what they say they are going to do. If they can't meet a deadline, they need to openly communicate that. It's imperative that, as a leader, you are clear in your expectations. If you find that you are unable to meet a deadline, make a meeting, or follow through on a promise, you need to be prepared to articulate clearly why as well.

When the Cat's Away, the Mice Will Play

I had just finished talking to my Marines about maintaining professional appearances and composure and not drinking alcohol in excess. I had also given special instructions to the two Marines that I relied on and trusted most. I asked them to represent me at the company party and be the example for the other Marines. In effect, I was putting them in charge, as I would not be able to attend. I articulated to them that this meant not treating the company event like a frat party. It meant maintaining military discipline, paying attention to the Marines' behavior throughout the night, and stepping in if they were starting to act out of character. They fully understood, and each Marine had given me their word that neither would have more than one drink at the company party, if they drank at all. These were two of the best Marines I had, and to date, they had not let me down. As I left work for the evening, I had a gnawing feeling that leaving the Marines with nine kegs of beer was going to be an issue, but I dismissed it. After all, the Marines were adults, and my expectations for them were clear. Plus, two of my most reliable and dependable Marines were in charge. What could go wrong?

It was the middle of the night when my phone started buzzing, startling me awake. It was my boss. Never a good sign. She was calling to let me know that a few of our Marines had overindulged and gotten into a verbal confrontation with two other people—two Marines who were higher in rank. Making matters worse, the confrontation took place in front *of everyone in the company. Nervous to hear the answer, I asked who the Marines were. At first I was shocked when she said it was my two most dependable and trusted direct reports. The two Marines I put in charge that evening. The two Marines who I had taken under my wing and invested time into grooming for increased responsibility. My shock quickly turned to anger as I remembered the conversation I had with them before I left. The two Marines completely disregarded everything I had taught them about leadership and setting a good example. Worse yet, they did the exact opposite of what I asked of them and were the ones who lost their composure.*

The next morning, I arrived at work early, hoping to get a head start on the day, and I saw my two direct reports outside my office. The door was locked, and they were sitting on the red bench, where you normally sat as you awaited punishment. The look in their eyes was clear; they knew they were in deep trouble and that they had lost all credibility with me and the other Marines in our unit. Their actions, over the course of only three hours, completely harmed their reputation and image as leaders. My ability to depend on both was gone as well. Even worse, as a result of their very public behavior, the other Marines that witnessed the altercation lost respect for these two as well. All in all, everything they had worked for was undone in the matter of one evening.

The Catch-22 of Being Dependable

Dependability isn't just a nice to have. It actually leads to better outcomes for you. For example, the more dependable you are, the more responsibility you will be given. No one wants to promote someone they can't rely on. Rather, a dependable person tends to gain more responsibility, either in their specific department or within the organization as a whole. "Dependable" becomes part of your brand and your reputation. It means you can work with less supervision and more autonomy. And the more consistent you are, the more dependable others will see you. The more dependable you are, the more responsibilities you take on, the more money you can make. These all sound like great things, right?

Yes, these are all great things and great for your career. The catch is, the more people who rely on you, the more work you are asked to take on, the less people think you need assistance because they trust in your abilities to get things done, and the more you end up feeling overwhelmed, stressed out, and dumped on. Do you see how it can quickly result in inconsistent results because you're trying to juggle so much?

We've both had this happen, especially early in our careers when we were first starting out. In fact, it tends to be quite common, even among our friends, and happens regardless of where you are in your career. For example, one of our closest friends was talking about how she's working seventy plus hours, including weekends, to try to keep up with her workload. She works for a mid-size brokerage firm and is viewed as highly dependable, both in her ability to keep up with new legal requirements as they pertain to the business and in her capacity to always deliver outstanding results. She routinely takes on one new client after another and gets pulled into various side projects because people know they can rely on her and her results. It got so bad at one point that when one of her colleagues left the company for a new job, rather than replacing his position, the work was divided among our friend and one other person in her department because the manager knew both were reliable. Our friend was starting to feel the physical and mental effects of working so many hours, and it was definitely starting to affect her work product.

The advice we gave our friend, and the advice that we would give to anyone in a similar situation, is to speak up. Your colleagues and manager aren't mind readers. They came to you for assistance because they trust you and rely on you. If you're feeling overwhelmed and your work is beginning to suffer, speak up. Do so in a respectful way aligned with your values, but definitely do so. It doesn't take away from your reputation as someone who is highly dependable. If anything, it adds to it because you don't want to compromise results.

Putting It into Practice

Dependability can definitely be developed as a leadership trait, one that will benefit you personally and professionally. Here are a few things you can start doing immediately to help.

Learn to say no. This is hard. We've both struggled with this at various points in our lives, both personally and professionally. We want to help. We want to be a good friend or a good coworker. We want people to think highly of us. But saying yes to everything and everyone helps no one at the end of the day. Being dependable isn't about saying yes all of the time. It's saying yes to the right things and using discretion when making commitments. Before saying yes, consider whether the commitment is a high priority for you. Then consider the timeline and deadlines. Are they doable? Also consider why you would be saying yes. Is it to appease the other person? Or is it something you are genuinely interested in doing? If the commitment isn't a priority for you and if you aren't committed, say no!

Don't make excuses. And definitely don't lie. If you've made a commitment and circumstances have changed, openly communicate and tell the other person why you are unable to keep your commitment. Perhaps you can even help find someone who is able to deliver in your place. When providing others with information or updates on the commitment, don't lie. Lying by omission is still a lie. Tell the truth about your progress and any roadblocks you may be encountering. Be honest about whether you will be able to meet the timeline or deadline. As a leader, most certainly don't play the blame game. Take accountability for any issues and work to come up with a plan to move forward.

Be on time. A common saying in the Marine Corps is "If you're not early, you're late." While you don't always have to be early everywhere you go, you do have to be on time. Showing up to meetings on time, dialing in to conference calls on time, arriving to dinner with friends on time all play into your reputation as a dependable leader. If you are notoriously late for everything, think about how you can get yourself on a better schedule to allow yourself to be on time. Sometimes at work, we are in constant back-to-back meetings where it feels like we are always showing up late to the next meeting. If you are the scheduler, try to make the meeting for twenty-five minutes instead of thirty, or fifty minutes instead of one hour. The extra time will not only allow you and others to be at their next commitment on time, but this will also give you a little time to mentally prepare for the next meeting so you can be more present.

Our ability to be viewed as dependable and to follow through on our commitments is important in our professional relationships and to our career trajectories. The ability to keep commitments and deliver results with integrity and honesty is critical to every aspect of our lives.

CHAPTER 4

INTEGRITY

Uprightness of character and soundness of moral principles.
The quality of truthfulness and honesty.

After returning from what would be my last deployment, I was transferred to Infantry Training Battalion (ITB), the next stop after boot camp for all Marines headed to infantry units. Here, I would lead a group of instructors to teach weapons use and tactics and combat survival to new Marines. These instructors were the best of the best in the infantry units of the Marine Corps.

It was about 5:00 p.m. on a Monday evening, and I had just pulled into my garage at home, ready to decompress from work, when my cell phone rang. It was the battalion Sergeant Major, the highest-ranking enlisted Marine in the battalion, asking what I knew about the recent weekend arrest of one of my newest instructors. After a brief pause, I answered with, "Absolutely nothing. What happened?"

For the next five minutes, he told me that the instructor's name appeared on the weekend police blotter. His offense? A DUI. Two thoughts ran through my mind. First, there's no way he did this. Maybe it was someone else with the same name because my instructor was really good at his job. Second, if this was him, why was I hearing about it two days later from my boss and not from my instructor directly? We talked for a few more minutes, and there was no doubt in my mind that it was, in fact, my instructor. I was fuming. This instructor had been in the Marine Corps long enough to know better. I told my boss that it looked like the instructor was trying to hide the incident, hoping we wouldn't find out. Before hanging up, we talked about next steps and what needed to happen.

Trying to keep my composure, yet still hoping it was all a mistake, I called my instructor. I told him I just got off the phone with my boss who mentioned the police blotter. Without any further prompting, he explained what had happened. He and a friend went out, and they had a few drinks. While he had only had two beers, his friend, on the other hand, had quite a few more and was in no shape to drive. Around 10:00 p.m., they left the bar. My instructor drove them to his house, which was five minutes away. As he turned onto his street, he saw the red and blue flashing lights. He was being pulled over for failure to come to a complete stop at a stop sign. The officer asked for license, insurance, and registration and then asked if my instructor had been drinking. He admitted to having two beers over the course of a few hours. The officer returned from his squad car, documents in hand, and asked the instructor to step outside the vehicle for a field sobriety test. Upon passing, a breathalyzer was administered. The instructor blew a 0.083, legally drunk in the state of California. He was arrested immediately for operating a vehicle while under the influence.

While I was glad that he was telling me the story, I couldn't help feeling like something was still missing. First, there was the obvious: two beers over the course of two hours and a 0.083 blood alcohol level. That didn't make sense. Second, and most importantly, why hadn't he said anything prior? I asked if he knew that he had to immediately notify me and the command of the incident. He said yes. So why hadn't he, then? Because he didn't think that the command would ever find out since the incident happened off base.

The next day, my instructor had to explain his actions to the colonel, the battalion commander of ITB (think CEO). It was a well-known fact that the colonel valued integrity above all else. In fact, less than one month prior, the colonel was meeting with my instructor about his leadership style and how it centered around integrity. And now here we were, talking about integrity again in a much different context.

Two days later, my boss and I were again standing in the colonel's office ready to inform my instructor of his punishment. As he walked in, I could see the disappointment written all over the colonel's face. He started the conversation by giving the definition of integrity, followed by the definition of cowardice. He rhetorically asked the instructor which best matched his actions. While the formal punishment proceedings had yet to begin, the colonel's choice words had already set the tone.

Then the proceedings began. The instructor took responsibility for his actions and admitted that he knew better. Not missing a beat, the colonel replied that, as a leader in the Marine Corps, he should have taken responsibility on Saturday night, when the incident occurred. He continued, comparing the instructor's actions to that of an adolescent child and not of a decorated combat veteran. The colonel then delivered the maximum punishment that he could impose, the instructor would have his pay reduced by half for two months. In addition, the instructor was essentially fired and would no longer be allowed to serve as an instructor. He couldn't be trusted, and with his integrity in question, it was best that he transfer out of the command immediately.

Much like in the business world, a leader's reputation precedes them. And in the Marine Corps, the former instructor's new boss would know exactly the type of Marine he was getting, one who didn't meet the Marine Corps's definition of integrity: "uprightness of character and soundness of moral principles. The quality of truthfulness and honesty."

In the Marine Corps, you can get "fired" from one job and move to another without losing your employment. In the business world, however, a lack of integrity can and will get you fired. In business, we would define integrity in much the same way the Marine Corps does. Both in the Marine Corps and in business, integrity is critical. In fact, based on our experience, integrity is so important that it's not uncommon for organizations to have it as one of their core values. However, there is a difference between an organization having integrity as a value and a leader having integrity. A value, written on a wall, a website, or piece of paper may not actually be how the company behaves. Think back to Enron.

Houston, Texas-based Enron was an electric and natural gas company in the early 2000s that employed nearly 30,000 employees and boasted revenues reportedly exceeding $101 billion. Enron's website listed four corporate values: respect, communication, excellence, and integrity. By late 2001, the behemoth filed for bankruptcy due to fraud and corruption, the revenue numbers had been doctored, a widely known practice inside of Enron. But they had integrity as a value. Where was the integrity as documents were being forged and numbers padded? Integrity, in this case, was lip service. It's what looked good to clients, politicians, and investors. But what about the leaders within Enron? Didn't they have integrity? In short, some of them did, like the whistleblower who brought the fraud and corruption to light. Not all the leaders did. If they had, perhaps the Enron scandal wouldn't have occurred.

When integrity is an organizational value, it's important to operationalize it and bring it to life and to answer questions, such as:

- How does our organization define integrity?
- What does it look like to have integrity in our organization?
- Why is integrity important to us?

Where most organizations fall short is not individualizing integrity. For example:

- What does integrity look like in my specific job?
- How does my team define integrity based on the work we do?
- What does integrity mean to me?

It is important that leaders define integrity for themselves and identify specific behavioral expectations associated with it. In addition, it's important to remember how we define integrity does not change from a professional to a personal setting. While the context may change, the meaning does not. Think back to Mike's instructor. Yes, integrity would have been notifying the command of the arrest and DUI on Saturday night. But integrity would also have been not driving while under the influence, which could have potentially caused serious harm to himself, his friend, and others on the road.

Components of Integrity

Take a moment and write down your definition of integrity. Below are a few universal components. There are many more, but we find these to be the most important. How many of these did your definition include?

Honesty. This one sounds simple—telling the truth at all times and not taking advantage of others. Yet, it can be hard for leaders to fully practice. This isn't because they are trying to be deceptive. Sometimes it's difficult to say the whole truth as it may hurt someone's feelings. So, instead, we only say the good parts. But being honest is more than focusing on the positive. It's about being discerning in what information you are sharing. Don't share unnecessary information and don't try and talk or dance around the point when needing to communicate difficult news. Just be respectful and think about what must be done in the best interest of everyone.

Respect to all. Whether in a personal or professional setting, we have all seen narrow-minded, insensitive, and outright-rude behavior from others. The outcome is hardly ever positive. A number of years back, Hema was working for a healthcare company where one of the members of the executive team threw a chair at his executive assistant because he didn't like what she had to say. While you would think this was a one-off bad-leader example, a few years later, at a different organization with a different executive team, one of the leaders had thrown a printer because he was angry that he wasn't getting his way. Luckily, in both instances, no one was hurt. Unfortunately, in both instances, respect was the last thing either of these leaders had for those around them. Being respectful to all is about assuming positive intent and giving people the benefit of the doubt, even if you don't agree with their viewpoints or opinions. Ask questions to clarify, try to understand, and be polite. Respect is a two-way street. If you are treating others respectfully, they should reciprocate.

Responsibility and trust. These two go hand-in-hand. We talked about them with regards to dependability and the same applies here, with integrity. Trust is built when you follow through, keep your promises and commitments, and do what you say you're going to do. Furthermore, trust is built when you take accountability and ownership of your actions and behaviors. Rather than saying, "trust me," show that you are truthful through your actions. Remember, your word is your bond. If you start to break promises and commitments, others will take notice. Not only will this hurt your reputation for dependability, but it will hurt how others view your integrity.

Selflessness. We've all heard the term "servant leadership," where the main goal of a leader is to serve. Along the same lines, selflessness is about facilitating the success of others, to serve them so they can succeed. A leader who is selfless understands that they may be on the losing end of that success sometimes. And that's okay. Think about the last time one of your employees left the company to pursue another job. The new job was a promotion, and you knew your current organization was unable to offer that type of promotion at this time. As a leader, were you happy for your employee to take this next step in their career or were you focused on asking why and how to get them to change their mind and stay? While difficult, a selfless leader knows and understands that a promotion for someone on their team, whether with your current organization or a new one, is a good thing and beneficial to that employee. Selflessness is important to integrity because it keeps the focus on doing the right thing, even if it may not be the right thing for you personally.

Moral courage. This one goes in tandem with a few of the others. Moral courage is speaking up, even when it's an unpopular opinion, or doing the right thing, even though it may be damaging to you.

This is where Mike's instructor fell short—he lacked the moral courage to admit that he was arrested because he knew it would hurt his career. Whether we lie or choose to tell the truth, there are always consequences for our actions. Having moral courage is also about asking others for their opinions and really listening to what they have to say. In leadership positions, this isn't always easy as we may not want to hear what our direct reports think about our leadership style or a recent decision we've made. But by having the courage to listen, we can grow in our leadership capacity and become better leaders. We will talk more about courage in Chapter 11.

Water is Good for the Body

Every night before bed in boot camp, we had to drink at least sixteen ounces of water to prepare us for whatever torture was scheduled the next day. The drill instructor would stand in the middle of the room and watch us as we finished our canteens. But they wouldn't just take our word that we had finished all of our water. Simultaneously, and on command, all ninety-eight recruits had to hold the canteen upside down over our heads.

So, there I stood one night, full canteen in hand, waiting for the command to drink. I heard the order and chugged until the canteen was empty. As I held the canteen upside down over my head, a few expected drops of water dripping down, I noticed the recruit across from me had his canteen right side up. This could only mean one thing; he hadn't finished his water and was hoping the drill instructor would not notice. Big mistake.

After a loud and witty one-liner, the drill instructor told the recruit to turn his canteen over. As water poured all over the recruit's face and onto the floor, the look on his face was one of complete defeat. Apparently he had only taken a few sips, as he was drenched. The drill instructor leaned in and whispered something to the soaked recruit. A whisper that was meant to be heard by everyone in the room—the recruit would be punished the following day for not having any integrity. To add insult to injury, the recruit had to clean up the water. As the drill instructor turned to walk away, I could see a faint crack of a smile.

The moral of the story? First, your actions speak volumes about your character. They speak to who you are, not only as a leader, but as a person. Second, keep the big picture in mind. The discomfort of drinking the water would have been better than the drill instructor and ninety-seven other recruits losing trust in the one recruit because he chose to lie.

Mike graduating from boot camp (February 16, 1996)

While we have listed five components of integrity, you may have a few more and that's okay. Everyone's definitions will be slightly different based on our own experiences. The goal is for leaders to actually have integrity. Collectively, when we have an organization of leaders with integrity, success follows.

Integrity in Leadership Leads to Better Business Outcomes

We all know that leadership is a critical factor in building organizational culture. The more integrity leaders have, the greater the ethical culture of the organization, the better the business performance. There are quite a few areas within an organization that see sustained improvement and success as a result of having integrity.

Stronger company culture. Leaders serve as role models; what they do, others emulate. So it shouldn't come as a surprise that if leaders have integrity, businesses on the whole are more ethical. When all employees have integrity in an organization, there is inherently more trust. This can result in increased flexibility in work arrangements, better communication, and better developmental opportunities, all resulting in overall growth of the individuals within the organization. A culture of ethics and compliance leads to better employee morale and engagement. Would you want to work for a company where you were always questioning whether your manager and the organization were doing the right thing? What would you do if your manager asked you to do something that went against your morals? Think about the toxic culture that would create and think about the misalignment that could cause. When integrity is prioritized, a culture of doing the right thing is created. Not only are employees less likely to engage in risky and unethical behavior, but they are also more likely to report any corruption or wrongdoing they witness.

Staying out of legal trouble. Legal issues are expensive. Fines and lawsuits add up, and when organizations experience legal trouble, the result can often lead to layoffs and bankruptcy. But, when organizations promote a culture of integrity and ethical behavior, they reap the rewards. The money that would be paid in legal fees is put back into the organization.

Attracting the right employees. Like many aspects of business, integrity is self-perpetuating. Organizations who value integrity and make it a priority, in turn, attract leaders who have integrity. Organizations that show they have a lack of integrity struggle to find the right talent. For example, a 2013 study of 480 firms across the top thirty-one exporting countries found that the firms that had integrity failings were less likely to attract and retain talented employees.[1]

Better reputations. Once an organization has an integrity failure, it becomes known. This is one reason why these organizations can't attract and retain top talent. But when organizations have a strong reputation, one without ethical corruption, they reap the benefits of that reputation in the form of revenue and capital. Would you buy from a brand where you had ethical concerns? If you said no, you aren't alone. In fact, 56% of Americans will stop buying from a brand they find unethical. The most common trait considered when determining whether a brand is ethical or not is how an organization treats its employees.[2]

---

[1] Paul Healy and George Serafeim, "An Analysis of Firms' Self-Reported Anticorruption Efforts." *The Accounting Review* 91, 2 (2016): 489-511.

[2] Lauren Bonetto, "56% of Americans Stop Buying from Brands They Believe are Unethical." Social and Lifestyle, Mintel Press Office, Published November 18, 2015, https://www.mintel.com/press-centre/social-and-lifestyle/56-of-americans-stop-buying-from-brands-they-believe-are-unethical.

Over the past few years, corporate social responsibility (CSR) reporting has gained momentum. CSR is a form of self-regulation and includes publicly reporting internal data on charitable giving and ethically oriented practices. Two areas generally included are accounting and auditing practices and ethical training. CSRs have become a source of information for consumers and prospective employees alike, because the more ethical an organization, the better their reputation.

Access to capital. In addition to increased revenue, organizations with higher integrity tend to see more capital at a lower cost. Not only do they have a lower-risk profile, making them more attractive to potential investors, but investors view them as having better leadership and more ethical policies and procedures, which all leads to a better potential for long-term success.

Sustained performance. Prioritizing profits over anything and everything else is not a good strategy. While there may be operating costs associated with creating a culture of integrity, the long-term benefits far outweigh the short-term costs. A 2014 study of 181 publicly traded US organizations found that those which proactively engaged in producing CSR reports outperformed their competitors in the long-term with regards to stock performance and accounting performance.[3]

We could go on and on about the personal and organizational benefits of having integrity. Research proves time and again that organizations that have leaders with integrity outperform their

---

[3] Robert G. Eccles, Ioannis Ioannou, and George Serafeim, "The Impact of a Corporate Culture of Sustainability on Corporate Behaviour and Performance," NBER Working Paper 17590, National Bureau of Economic Research, Cambridge, MA: March 2014.

peers. Speaking from firsthand experience, Hema can attest to the fact that organizations without integrity are just bad places to be. Early in her career, she worked for a small brokerage company that was seeing phenomenal growth and attracting large Fortune 500 clients. One night, she figured out why. It was the evening before a big presentation was due to a large prospective client. Hema finished up the presentation and sent it to her boss, along with the CEO of the company. A short time later, she received an email asking for some of the examples to be altered—to show a higher cost-savings than what would be realized. She didn't feel comfortable doing this, but the CEO made the updates anyway. Since she was still new to the business world, she was unsure of what to do. She knew it wasn't right and she didn't view her boss or the CEO in the same way after this incident. About a year later, the FBI raided the organization. The charge was fraud and antitrust violations. Luckily, Hema had already left the organization. But when she was contacted for her statement, Hema told the truth. She knew that her friends would lose their jobs and the organization would most likely have to close its doors. At the end of the day, the statement Hema provided was minor in comparison to what was actually occurring within the organization. Regardless, while difficult, telling the truth was the right thing to do. The lesson stays with her to this day—if it doesn't feel right, it probably isn't. Having integrity is standing up for what is right.

Putting It into Practice

Unlike some of the other leadership traits, integrity can be a hard one to learn. You either have it or you don't. However, even if you have it, your actions may not be fully aligned. Here are a few things you can do to ensure your actions are aligned with your character.

Conduct a self-audit. Think about other leaders you admire. Why do you admire them? What traits do they possess that you would like to emulate? How successful are you at emulating those traits today? If you fall short in a particular area, try to understand why that may be. Conducting a self-audit is a good place to begin, as you need to know your starting point. Think about the components of integrity we mentioned above. Use these areas to help guide you in taking an honest look at your own actions and behaviors.

Ask others. We each have blind spots, areas of ourselves that we can't see. We may think we know how we are perceived, but we really should know for sure. Ask coworkers who you trust or friends who know you well. Find out what you do well and what's working. Find out what you could do better and where you may need to spend some time focusing. A good person to ask is your manager. During your next one-on-one meeting, ask your manager for their opinion and be open about why you are asking. People tend to be honest if they know it's for self-improvement.

Intentionally pause. Occasionally, and without meaning to, we may make excuses for why we did or did not do something. It's almost like a defense mechanism, as we want to protect ourselves. Doing so can sometimes cause us to act without integrity. For example, if you make a mistake, rather than making an excuse, pause and own it. Then work to fix it. This intentional pause allows you to gather your thoughts and speak from a place of honesty and integrity. It's also okay to be vulnerable. Remember, being a leader isn't about being right or perfect all of the time.

Integrity is about practicing what you preach and holding true to your core values. It is the key to your reputation and can open many doors for you, personally and professionally.

CHAPTER 5

DECISIVENESS

*The ability to make decisions promptly and
to announce them in a clear, forceful manner.*

E very morning, Marine Corps leaders around the world need
to provide accountability reports to the leaders of their units.
These reports are consolidated and ultimately are submitted
to the Pentagon. These reports are used by the Pentagon to better
understand how many Marines are located in what part of the world
should military action be needed. These accountability reports are
required twice daily for deployed units, 7:00 a.m. and 5:00 p.m.
While I did these reports for years, it wasn't until the second month
of my final deployment that they would lead to one of the biggest
decision-making mistakes of my career.

My department leaders were not providing their accountability
reports to me on time, and if the reports were submitted on time,
the information was often inaccurate. In turn, I was submitting
late or incorrect information to the battalion, which was raising
concerns about my effectiveness to lead.

The problems with the reports persisted even after I repeatedly
addressed the issues with my department leaders. I tried to allow my

leaders to make the necessary adjustments and correct the problem. But finally I knew I had to take control and make a decision as to what I was going to do, a decision that would frustrate every single person in my unit. Finally, at my wit's end, I ordered all personnel in my unit to be present at 5:30 a.m. on the flight deck of the ship. Here, the department leaders could account for each person while I supervised. I knew when I issued the order that it was not going to be received well and that I would be the villain. But it was the only option I was left with. The deciding factor was being pulled aside by my supervisor to discuss the importance of timely and accurate reporting of the accountability report. This discussion eliminated any concern I had about the Marines' discomfort.

For the first couple of weeks, I felt that solid progress had been made and that my point had been received by the department leaders. They knew why accurate accountability was so important, and I was considering allowing the department leaders to conduct accountability on their own again.

Until one morning when I saw several Marines looking disheveled and unshaven. I pulled the department leaders aside to inquire about these issues. Making matters worse, while I was talking to the leaders, I saw a Marine running to join his department group. The problem? I was told that every person was present. I was absolutely furious. The department leader tried to explain why the Marine was late, but I didn't want to hear it. I was angry and didn't want my leadership questioned by my boss. So I made an impulsive, knee-jerk reaction that would ultimately lead to losing the confidence and trust of my department leaders and having to work to gain it back.

At 5:30 a.m. every morning, in addition to accountability, I was going to personally inspect each Marine to ensure their appearance was in line with Marine Corps standards. My impulsive decision led to more work for me, awkwardness for my Marines, and a demonstration of my lack of confidence in my department leaders, in full view of the Marines who reported directly to them. Yes, I made a decision. But it was a flawed decision and one for which I didn't think through the consequences. My Marines avoided me out of fear that I would find a discrepancy and implement some type of punishment. My department leaders were annoyed. And my boss was still questioning the effectiveness of my leadership, this time for different reasons. My Marines deserved better.

I had to fix the wrongdoing and backtrack on my decision. I met with my department leaders so we could have an honest discussion and I could hear their side and they mine in order to come to a better decision for all. Finally, I amended my decision, taking into account all information. We were all aligned and working together.

Decisiveness isn't just about making a decision, like I did. It's about making the best decision with the information available. That implies that, as a leader, it's important to listen to others, especially if the decision affects them. I was true, however, to the Marine Corps's definition of decisiveness: "the ability to make decisions promptly and to announce them in a clear, forceful manner." The last part, "in a...forceful manner," may work for the Marine Corps but most certainly doesn't work in business. Don't get us wrong; it's been used in organizations across the world by leaders who are often described as dictatorial, defensive, angry, selfish, and a whole host of other far-from-positive adjectives.

In Chapter 1, we talked about judgment and how to exercise good judgment to make good decisions. One critical aspect of being an effective leader is the ability to make decisions. All too often, we come across leaders who cannot decide on a course of action or even choose between two options. The CEO of one of our large clients in the aerospace industry unfortunately falls into this category. During the COVID-19 pandemic, his employees and members of the executive team were looking to him for guidance and direction on what to do regarding hiring.

Would there be a hiring freeze or not? After meeting with his Chief Human Resources Officer (CHRO) and other leaders on his team, he was still unable to make a decision. Instead, he asked his CHRO to have her team meet with every leader regarding every open position to see whether the position was necessary and, if so, whether it was critical enough to hire immediately. Of course, when posed with these questions, the majority of leaders stated their positions were both necessary and highly critical. This exercise took four weeks to complete, in which time new employees were still being hired; some recruiters and hiring managers were still interviewing while others purposely slowed down, and the organization was still no closer to a final decision. When presented with the information, the CEO was still not able to make a decision. Fast-forward six more weeks and a decision still didn't exist. The CEO's leadership team lost confidence in his ability to make decisions and the employees, who were awaiting direction, lost confidence in their leaders to influence a decision. The point here is the inability to be decisive has ripple effects that can be felt throughout the organization and can ultimately hurt your organization's culture, your team's trust and confidence in you, and your reputation as a leader.

What Makes a Decisive Leader?

Think about buying a car. Buying a car is a difficult and costly decision. I'm sure you consider make, model, color, features, new or used, financing, safety, consumer reports, and on and on. What is your thought process in making your decision? What ultimately leads you to make the final decision? How do you feel about your decision? Do you regret it?

Hema's dad was recently in this position. He'd been talking about buying a new car for some time. He'd done his research and even test-drove various makes and models before settling on his final choice. He got a great deal on a luxury car and traded in his old one. A few days after he purchased the car, he called and said he missed his old car, but he liked his new one. It would just take time to get used to.

He made a decision to get a new car, but he was still questioning whether it was the *right* decision.

It's often thought that leaders need to make the right decision all the time. That always making the best decisions is how leaders become great. This isn't necessarily the case. According to the CEO Genome Project, one of the largest studies designed to determine the traits of successful CEOs, the ability to decide with speed and conviction was one of the four top behaviors that effective CEOs possess.[4] Notice that this didn't include the ability to make the right decisions. That's because making the wrong decision is better than making no decision at all.

---

[4] Elena Botelho et al., "What Sets Successful CEOs Apart," Harvard Business Review, May–June 2017, 70–77.

Critical Decisions Can't be Rushed

I felt like I was in the Twilight Zone. My battalion commander had just asked me a question, and for the life of me, I could not make a decision. I had a key position that had to be immediately filled or there would be negative cascading consequences, resulting in missed deadlines. I was presented with two choices, and neither were ideal. Both had their pros and cons. Did I select the person who knows the job and who was currently doing the same job in another department but whose performance was lacking and whose attitude was poor? Or did I select the person who didn't know how to do the job, but who already worked in my department, who I trusted, and who performed well in his current job, with the hope that he did well in the new job?

The position I had to fill was the lead instructor for my training company at Infantry Training Battalion (ITB). This role was responsible for scheduling the training events for the students (new Marines who were just graduating boot camp), coordinating medical support, and everything in between. The position also had considerable leadership and supervisory responsibilities, so I had to choose carefully. I wasn't prepared when the battalion commander asked for my decision because I needed more time to think and I wanted to talk to the two individuals first. Clearly seeing the distant and confused look on my face, the battalion commander gave me four days to make my decision.

During those four days, I observed how both candidates interacted with their peers and with the students. I also observed how each acted during their downtime, away from the students. This was critically important to me because this spoke to their passion for the job and their initiative as a leader: Were they comfortable with the status quo and doing the bare minimum, or did they want to make the people around them better? As it turned out, this final element, what they did during their downtime, would ultimately be the deciding factor. My internal candidate was always pushing his group of students to improve, often teaching them additional techniques to prepare them for real world missions. He showed genuine care and concern for his students and for his peers. The external candidate was the opposite. He was focused on texts or playing games on his phone rather than the training he was supposed to be observing and leading. The only times he would be engaged were when a senior Marine was in the area.

I was ready to make my decision. I discussed it with my boss, and we were ready to inform the battalion commander. We went with the internal candidate, the one without the relevant experience, but the one who was engaged and motivated to make those around him better. I was confident that he could handle the additional responsibilities. As for the external candidate? I explained what I had observed and what led to my decision. The battalion commander was not surprised by the decision or by my comments. In fact, unbeknownst to me, the battalion commander was looking for another perspective before he made his decision on where to transfer the external candidate.

The bottom line: when faced with an important decision, taking the extra time to really think before acting is essential.

The good news is, most decisions, both in life and in business, can be modified and reversed. Hardly anything is permanent. We're talking business here, not healthcare or medical outcomes where the risks of making the wrong decision are very real. Most effective and great leaders realize that they aren't always going to make the right decision. They know that they will make a wrong decision here and there. If that's the case, then why do so many of us fret about our options before making a decision? Because we're scared. The fear of failure is real, especially early on in our careers. As we progress, we fear making the wrong decisions. This fear can become paralyzing and hurt our reputations. So, how can we overcome fear? Through courage. (Let's come back to that in Chapter 11.)

So, if always making the right decision isn't a characteristic of a decisive leader, then what makes a leader decisive?

Decisive leaders are accountable for their actions and their decisions. They understand the ripple effects their decisions may have on others and on the organization. But, they are committed and will follow through to own the outcome. They do what they say they are going to do. Once a decision is made, they see it through to execution. This doesn't mean that if new information comes to light, they don't adjust. It just means they don't pull back. Think back to dependability. A decisive leader is dependable. They can be counted on to make a decision and see it through.

Decisive leaders build trust through their actions. There is nothing worse than someone saying they are going to do something and then not doing it! This is even more so true for leaders. Leaders become leaders because others look to them as trusted advisors of sorts. The need to make decisions goes hand-in-hand with being a leader. As a leader, if you say you are going to do something, make sure you do it. If, for whatever reason, you can't follow through or your decision needs to be completely changed, you should explain why.

Decisive leaders are not impulsive. They are deliberate. Impulsive leaders jump the gun and make a reactionary decision. Often enough, they go back and change their minds frequently. Have you ever been in a situation where you had to make a quick decision, you didn't think it through all the way, and later you realize you made the wrong decision and there was a better option? For the most part, these decisions are not life or death, so going back to change them is okay. But, as a leader, you need to be more deliberate. When faced with a situation that requires an immediate decision, but one that isn't as straightforward as you may think, ask for even ten minutes to think about it. This allows you the ability to avoid being reactionary and moves you into being more deliberate about your decision.

Decisive leaders don't act on emotion. Impulsive leaders do. Decisive leaders understand that emotions can often distort thinking and influence behavior. They also know that emotions do play a part in decision-making. However, instead of reacting, decisive leaders balance their emotions with facts. They use logic and experience to arrive at a decision and they use their emotions as a gut check: Does the decision feel right? There most certainly is a place for emotion in decision-making. However, decisions should be based in facts, which makes explaining why you came to the decision you did a bit easier as well. Imagine talking to your manager about your performance. On the most recent review, they scored you a three out of five. In the comments section, and in talking to you, their reason was "Because I felt like you were doing an okay job." There is no mention of the fact that you are newer to your position. No mention of the fact that you took the lead on a project that was ultimately canceled as business priorities shifted. No mention of the fact that you picked up the workload of a team member who left. Instead of those facts, the reason was based on how someone felt about you.

Decisive leaders are always moving forward. Being a decisive leader is a bit like walking on a tightrope. You have to navigate a fine line between making a decision quickly and taking your time to weigh the facts. Move too quickly and you could do more harm than good. Move too slowly and stall progress. Decisive leaders navigate this balance daily to keep moving forward. They tap into their experience and knowledge to help make a decision quickly when necessary. But, they know their limits and understand the gravity of certain decisions and, therefore, know when to slow down.

If you haven't noticed already, being decisive relies quite a bit on experience and knowledge and making the best decision with the information available. However, we all have the ability to really build the decisiveness muscle, regardless of where we are in our careers.

Building the Decisiveness Muscle

Some people are just born with the ability to make quick decisions. Self-admittedly, Mike is not one of those people. He's a processor. Early in his career, he also wanted to make sure he said the right thing or made the right decision. As he progressed throughout his career, he realized that he needed to be more decisive. One way he did this was by tapping into the knowledge of his Marines. He knew that the collective knowledge was better than just his own. He sought out information to help in the decision-making process. Another way he did this was by asking questions. He sought out information that would help him in his decision-making. He had to strike a balance between analysis paralysis and obtaining enough information to make a well-informed decision. Overall, it took some time, but the more he practiced these techniques, the easier it became.

Confidence and self-assurance are also keys to building the decisiveness muscle. There is a fine line here between confident and cocky. When communicating decisions or articulating messages, decisive leaders are clear in their intent. Others know the direction; they know the why. This is also another way to build trust. The important note here is to remain humble in your interactions. Others who look to you as a leader do so because you are approachable and admit when you may not know something, yet are confident in your own abilities. No one likes a cocky leader, and we can all name at least one we know.

The CEO for one of our academic clients falls squarely in this category. While he was decisive, he also believed he was the smartest person in the room. He tended to make the right decision about 90% of the time, decisions that led to increased success for the organization. However, the manner in which he would communicate these decisions or how to execute his decisions was more dictatorial and arrogant than humble and confident. The employees ended up avoiding him when he would walk around the office and wouldn't openly discuss their thoughts or ideas with him, even when prompted. So, while he may have been decisive, this CEO was certainly not a true leader.

Finally, start to understand your tendencies: Do you make decisions on data or a gut feeling the majority of the time? One way to be more decisive in the future is to examine the past. In Chapter 1, when we talked about judgment, we mentioned understanding your default bias. The same is true here. Basing decisions on your gut or on data are not inherently bad. Being aware of how you usually make decisions will help you find a better balance with how you *should* make decisions. For example, if you usually rely on your instinct, try to have some data to back up a decision. If you usually rely on data, think about how the decision makes you feel and whether you would make the same decision if you were to consider your experience or your feeling.

Putting It into Practice

The good news is, there are many things you can start doing today to help you be a more decisive leader in the future.

Trust your instincts. Once a decision is made, decisive leaders are slow to change their minds. This isn't because they are stubborn, although some of them certainly may be. It's because they trust their instincts. These instincts are built on a depth of experience they can tap into. It's also built on knowledge, because they are lifelong learners. To trust your instincts more, broaden your experience by asking to be put on special projects or working toward a promotion or pursuing a passion that is of interest. In addition, continue reading books and articles on relevant topics to expand your knowledge. Then, when the time comes to make decisions, tap into what you know to help guide you.

Prioritize effectively. Think about each aspect of your role. This could be your role at work or your role at home. Which parts of your role require you to make urgent and quick decisions and which parts allow you a little bit more time? Of the parts that require an immediate decision, what resources do you need to tap into when making those decisions? Each urgent decision may require a different set of resources based on the type of decision being made. For example, if the decision involves people, you may need to think about your past experience with the person and your past experiences in similar situations. If the decision is more process-based, you may need to tap into industry best practices and articles or books that provide the best solution for your problem. Decisiveness isn't about a one-size-fits-all approach. It's about making the best decision for the particular circumstance.

Be agile. All leaders know that circumstances change and nothing is certain. They know that their decision may or may not be the right one, but they need to make a decision and adjust as necessary. Agility allows leaders to assess the situation, both strategically and tactically, and change their course of action based on new information. Decisive leaders know that circumstances do, in fact, change and that there is a level of uncertainty as to the actual outcome of a situation based on a decision they have made. They also know that sometimes you can't have all of the information you may want or need in order to make a decision. The aerospace CEO we mentioned earlier is not agile in his decision-making capabilities. COVID-19 was unexpected, it was still early in the pandemic, and he needed as much information as possible in order to make a decision (which he didn't even end up making) rather than understanding the ebb and flow his decision might need to make as circumstances changed. To be more agile, start to get comfortable with information that is "good enough" versus perfect. This will allow you to make a decision versus stalling until you have everything you need.

We can all agree that decisiveness as a leadership trait is critical in every organization around the world. Being decisive comes easier to some than it does others. The good news is, you can definitely learn to be more decisive by tapping into your confidence, strengths, and experiences. The more you practice, the easier it becomes.

CHAPTER 6

TACT

The ability to deal with others in a manner that will maintain good relations and avoid offense. More simply stated, tact is the ability to say and do the right thing at the right time.

I was working in the embassy in Berlin, preparing for an upcoming audit when my supervisor walked into my office. We were close friends, so I knew the look on his face; he was irate. He shut the door and said we had to talk in a tone that signified 'supervisor to subordinate' versus friend to friend.

He told me that the Marine who was responsible for tracking the ammunition supply was not correctly doing his job, as there was a significant error on the most recent tracking report. The error was only discovered when my supervisor was asked to approve and sign this report. Being thorough, my supervisor did a spot check between what appeared on the report and compared that to the actual ammunition supply. When the two did not match, my supervisor asked the Marine why there was a discrepancy. The Marine fumbled in his response, leading my supervisor to believe the Marine was being dishonest.

As my supervisor was explaining the situation to me, followed by his opinion on how to punish this Marine (which was to send

69

him back to the US), I felt tense and found myself wanting to defend the Marine. For starters, my supervisor wasn't a Marine. He worked for a branch of the State Department that oversaw the Marines within the embassy. As such, he had zero authority to punish my Marine. That decision was reserved to the Marine Corps or the ambassador, who was the only person who could send a Marine home, essentially firing him. Second, I knew my Marines better than my supervisor did. I couldn't believe that the Marine in question would intentionally forge paperwork and then lie about it.

This was definitely a complicated and delicate situation that required diplomacy and finesse. Instead of reacting and acting out of emotion, I let him finish his story. When he was done, I told him I understood his position and asked him to give me the opportunity to talk to the Marine before taking any further action. I also casually mentioned that he intimidated many of the Marines, hoping he would understand that this could be the reason the Marine fumbled when answering his question. If nothing else, this at least eased the tension and de-escalated the situation as he cracked a smile.

After my supervisor left, I went to find the Marine in question to better understand his perspective. It was important to me that he felt comfortable talking to me about the situation and knew that I hadn't picked sides, especially as it was known how close my supervisor and I were. I could sense that he was nervous and a little worried, especially as he was early in his Marine career. I had to be careful that I said the right things and conveyed the right tone with my body language and facial expressions, which, for me, can be difficult as my feelings are depicted on my face. He started to calm down, feel more comfortable, and opened up about what had happened. As it turned out, the error in question had occurred two months prior and was missed on both of the months' reports. This Marine noticed the error initially but had simply forgotten to submit the correction paperwork. I then asked about his reaction when he was confronted by my supervisor. He said he was scared and nervous, and therefore, he stuttered when answering. Left with little doubt that the Marine was telling the truth, I had to have a hard discussion with my supervisor.

Walking into his office, I was slightly nervous because I had to take a very careful approach in explaining the whole story. I had to keep my tone, my words, and my emotions in check. As I began explaining in a calm and even-toned manner, I could see that he was receptive. I went on to explain that the fumbling or stuttering was not a sign of lying. The Marine was intimidated. In fact, in my first few interactions with the Marine, he did the same thing. Satisfied that it was all a misunderstanding, my supervisor deferred to me on whether to take any corrective action against the Marine. By remaining calm and staying positive, I was able to maintain my friendship with my supervisor and de-escalate the situation.

In the Marine Corps, tact is defined as: "the ability to deal with others in a manner that will maintain good relations and avoid offense. More simply stated, tact is the ability to say and do the right thing at the right time." In his interactions with his supervisor, Mike was the epitome of this definition. Whether in the Marine Corps or in the business world, it can be difficult to remain tactful in stressful situations. Luckily, Mike was able to do so and reach a positive outcome at the end of the day.

The business world defines tact in much the same way as the Marine Corps. One word that often shows up in business as it relates to tact is *"diplomacy."* The art of being diplomatic is critical, especially as you advance as a leader in your career. All eyes are on you, and people are watching and paying close attention to not only what you say, but how you say it. There's a tendency to scrutinize the actions of leaders as well as mimic the actions of leaders. If a leader can do it, it must be okay, so I'm going to do it too! Think about a great leader you've known. What was their communication style like, especially when giving difficult news? Chances are, they were diplomatic and had tact in how they delivered the news. If they were aggressive or rude in any way, we doubt you would think of them as a great leader.

Tact is an important leadership trait in both our personal and professional lives. It can also be closely tied to our values of respect and integrity.

Why is Tact so Important?

First, and most importantly, it speaks to your brand and reputation. You can be the smartest person in your department, maybe even in the entire organization, but if you can't communicate with empathy and convey truthful yet difficult information to others in a respectful way that takes into account their feelings, then it doesn't matter how smart you are. You will be viewed as someone who not only lacks tact but also someone who may be in misalignment with the organization's values and culture. An executive for one of our technology clients is a prime example of this. He went to Harvard for his undergraduate degree and Stanford for his graduate degree. He has an ability to pick things up quickly and retains information easily. He is smart;

there is no question about that. But his leadership team is constantly complaining about how he comes across in team meetings and in one-on-ones. He's been described as aggressive, passive-aggressive, a bully, and a jerk. When asked to explain various statistics he's created or diagrams he's made, his go-to response generally is, "I'm too busy and don't have time to deal with you." Or when he does finally concede to explain his creations, it's often done with an air of arrogance and phrases such as, "Intelligent people can pick this up quickly." He had previously discussed a potential promotion with the CEO, yet his behavior was ultimately the reason he was being passed over for that promotion. When told why he wasn't getting the promotion, the CEO mentioned that he didn't possess tact; he simply didn't know how to communicate in a manner that maintained strong relationships.

Another reason tact is important is because it helps you build and maintain strong relationships with peers, other leaders, and really anyone around you. When a leader has tact, they have the ability to convey difficult information in a way that helps the other person improve versus making them feel inferior. This ability is really important when you manage people. Performance discussions are just one place where we see tact (or a lack thereof) on full display. In this case, tact is the ability to talk about an area of improvement or a failure while keeping the best interests of the other person in mind. For example, if during a performance discussion, your manager blurted out that you failed to meet a critical deadline and continued on for five minutes about how your failure had other ramifications without giving you an opportunity to speak, what would that do to your relationship with your manager? If it was already rocky, we're sure this would only make it worse. However, if during this performance discussion your manager instead said, "I see you missed a critical deadline. As you know, that deadline was really important to the entire project. I know there have been a lot of moving pieces. Help me understand a bit better what happened," chances are you'd respond a lot differently to this. The goal for your manager was to maintain the good relationship you two have while talking openly and honestly about your missing a deadline.

Lastly, the ability to communicate with tact affects your career. This is the by-product of the first two reasons mentioned—brand and reputation—and the ability to maintain strong relationships. Very rarely do people who bully or tear down others get promoted. We're sure it happens. In fact, we know it happens. But, for the most part, these people are asked to leave the organization. At some point, their behavior catches up with them. The reverse is true as well. If you are a leader who has built a strong reputation centered around your ability to maintain good relationships, especially when encountering uncomfortable situations, others view you more as a leader and believe you have the capabilities to handle more complex and strategic matters, in addition to effectively managing people.

Diplomacy 101

While in a meeting with all of the senior department leaders at the embassy in Berlin, I was put on the spot by the Ambassador. He had just asked me to coordinate my Marines to act as doormen at an event he was holding. My initial reaction was "absolutely not." This was not an authorized use of the Marines. But before reacting and blurting out a response, I had to think about the words I needed to use to clearly articulate my point without offending the Ambassador. Not wanting to draw the silence out in the room any longer and knowing all eyes were on me, I asked if I could connect with him after the meeting to iron out the details. The goal was to avoid an international incident in front of senior ranking State Department officials. This strategy also gave me enough time to think of an alternative way the Marines could support the ambassador's event, maintaining my relationship with him in the process.

Immediately after the meeting, I met with the ambassador. He told me that he was a huge supporter of the Marines and wanted to showcase them at a big event he was hosting. His intentions were good. His approach was what I needed to address. I started by saying that I was flattered and honored by his comments. However, I was short-staffed, and therefore the Marines would not be able to support his event in the capacity he was hoping for. Before he had an opportunity to react, I quickly followed up with an alternative plan, allowing the ambassador to showcase the Marines without violating any rules and regulations and allowing me to have enough Marines to still effectively do their jobs. Instead of my Marines, I would stand next to the ambassador in my uniform and greet guests. In addition, Hema would also attend, which sealed the deal. He was thrilled, and I was able to maintain a great relationship with the ambassador. Now I just had to tell Hema…

How to Be More Tactful

It's obvious why tact is so important. It seems like some people are born with the people-pleaser gene, while others are born with the gene for always needing to prove they are better than others. The good news is, most of us are somewhere in between, depending on the situation. Regardless of whether you've been a leader for decades or are newer in your career, we all have the ability to learn how to be more tactful.

Build emotional intelligence (EQ). It's not a coincidence that we started here. If you aren't communicating tactfully, most likely it's for one of two reasons. First, you simply don't know how you are coming across to others, or second, you know and don't care. We're not going to focus on the second reason other than to say this book won't help you. We're going to focus on the first reason, which is ultimately caused by a lack of self-awareness. Self-awareness is part of EQ, the ability to understand and use your emotions to achieve positive communications with others. As part of EQ, self-awareness is the ability to be self-reflective and to know and understand how your thoughts, feelings, and actions are perceived by others. In addition, it's about knowing when to course-correct based on those perceptions. The ability to be diplomatic, especially when in uncomfortable or awkward situations falls squarely in this arena. A leader with self-awareness is acutely aware of how they need to control their feelings and emotions in stressful situations, especially when dealing with other people. They often lead with empathy and understanding rather than accusations and negativity.

Another component of EQ is effectively managing relationships. Leaders with a high EQ know how to inspire others through developing and maintaining good relationships. They also have social awareness, which allows them to pick up on the emotional cues of others and understand and respond accordingly. Think back to the executive at the technology company, the one who was being passed over for a promotion. How socially aware or self-aware do you think they were? How high do you think their EQ was, even though their IQ was very high? This executive lacked EQ. They were unable to effectively communicate in awkward or stressful situations and couldn't control their own emotions, causing them to not be tactful and to come across as rude and condescending.

Start building your EQ by responding and not reacting. When you act on and lead with your emotions, tact tends to go out the window. Also, be an active listener. In Chapter 1 we talked about three levels of listening. This is a great place to practice level-three listening. Rather than waiting for your chance to respond, be sure you understand what is being said first. This can help minimize conflict. Lastly, learn to empathize with others. This shouldn't be confused with sympathy. Empathy is the ability to understand someone else's feelings as if we were having those same feelings. Sympathy is really about taking on someone else's feelings as if they were our own. EQ is about understanding other people's emotions and responding accordingly.

De-escalate situations. Tact is very useful for conflict resolution. Conflicts tend to escalate because we allow our emotions to cloud our decision-making. But by being tactful, we can remove blame, thereby relieving some of the tension that was created. It's not about the blame game. In these situations, use "I" versus "you." These statements can be things like, "Here is what I'm hearing you say," or "Help me understand…" Even when giving feedback, these statements can sound like, "Next time, I think your presentation would be better if you explained your graphics a bit more. I had to go over those slides a few times." These statements don't put the other person on the defensive, and instead, you are taking ownership of your feelings. Tact is about choosing your words carefully because you know they can influence how a message is perceived.

A tactful leader says and does the right thing at the right time. In other words, a leader who possesses tact can read the room. They know the appropriate response based on the situation. They use their judgment to determine the best response, which can even be no response at all. As an example, a team meeting is not the best place to have a performance discussion with one of your employees. It sounds simple enough, yet many leaders get caught up in the moment and let their emotions overtake their response. Where you are, who you're with, and who is around you all need to be taken into consideration before speaking.

One note of caution before we move on. Communicating with tact shouldn't be used as an excuse for not doing your job. Oftentimes, leaders don't want to give constructive feedback or negative news, so they deflect or avoid it altogether. Even worse, they circle around the whole truth, sugarcoating the message or dancing around it. Being tactful isn't about avoiding information to spare someone else's feelings. It's about delivering the difficult news in a professional and respectful manner. Furthermore, deflecting or not being entirely truthful does nothing for your relationship with the person you are communicating with. In fact, it could hurt your relationship. For example, if you have allergies and your coworker who sits next to you wears a lot of cologne or perfume, exacerbating your allergies, what do you do? If you make blanket statements such as, "My allergies sure are acting up" or "I used to wear a lot of perfume/cologne, but not so much anymore due to my allergies," have you actually communicated anything to your coworker about their perfume and your allergies? The answer is no. They will continue wearing their scent, and you will continue with allergies and feeling angry over your coworker's use of perfume/cologne. The point here is to say, don't use tact to *avoid* difficult situations. Use tact to strengthen relationships when in those difficult situations.

Putting It into Practice

Tact as a leadership trait is vitally important, especially if you want to advance in your career. The good news is, you can learn to be more tactful. Below are a few things you can start doing today.

Think before you speak. This shouldn't come as a surprise. How many times have you said something that you wish you could take back? Things you may have said in the heat of the moment or without thinking first? When we lead with emotion, we react first and speak before we think. Instead, use the intentional pause we've mentioned previously. Use the pause to gather your thoughts and formulate what you're going to say and how you're going to say it. Allow yourself the time to be thoughtful in your approach, as this will also benefit you and your career. For example, if you disagree with something your manager says, don't be quick to jump the gun and blurt out, "That's not true at all." Instead, think of a few reasons why you disagree. Turn the situation into a conversation and take it as an opportunity to learn more about why your manager may feel the way they do and to explain why you feel the way you do. Also think about your timing. Remember, a tactful leader says and does the right thing at the right time. Before speaking, consider your environment. Talking about how excited you are about your recent promotion may not be the best conversation to have with someone who just lost their job.

Avoid office politics. The quickest and easiest way to not be tactful is taking part in office gossip and office politics. Instead, when you find yourself in a negative situation, tactfully deflect the negativity. Rather than joining a conversation about the recent alcohol-fueled antics at the holiday party, gently change the conversation or politely remove yourself from the conversation altogether. You can also be tactful in correcting the gossip: "I'm sorry you heard that about Brian. I spoke to him last week, and he mentioned it was just a rumor that he was getting fired."

How you say something is just as important as what you say. How many times have you thought, "It's not what you said, it's how you said it that made me react like I did?" We've certainly said that a time or two ourselves. The truth is, sometimes it's easy for people to see our lack of tact in our facial expressions, body language, and even in the specific and often critical words that we're using. The eye roll, the crossed arms, or even a sigh all convey your impatience, even though your words may be saying, "It's okay, take your time." Just like we mentioned in Chapter 1 with judgment, your body language sends a clear message and sets the tone for a conversation. Before you speak, think about your posture and hand placement and work to control your facial expressions so they are more aligned with what you are saying.

Tact isn't the first trait that comes to mind when talking about leadership. Oftentimes, it's not even in the top five. The truth is, the ability to communicate in a tactful manner is often what distinguishes a great leader from a good one.

CHAPTER 7

INITIATIVE

Taking action in the absence of orders.

Where in the world is she?

I needed to find Hema, and quickly, as time was of the essence. I asked over the radio if anyone had eyes on her but heard nothing. Then I turned the corner and saw her lying face down on the ground, hands over her head, with four rifles pointed directly at her. I stood there watching intently as my Marines attempted, and fumbled with, handcuffing her. Having seen enough, I told the Marines to let her go and that the drill was over. Hema was not my concern. She was fine. My Marines, on the other hand, needed help after that sloppy performance.

The Marines, myself included, all performed our duties during the drill. We followed directions. However, we needed to be more efficient and communicate more effectively. In the scenario, Hema had gained access into the embassy illegally and was trying to access classified information. We had to find and detain her as quickly as possible, while preventing the theft of classified material. If Hema had been a real intruder, or worse, an armed intruder, the Marines and I would have been in trouble. For the safety of every employee in the embassy, I had to make some adjustments to our training.

I thought about the critical aspects that we had to improve upon. Our internal communication, tactical movements, and use of technology were all lacking. Making matters worse, the Marines were not completely engaged and present in the moment. They were simply going through the motions. I had to make significant changes to our procedures and make the drill more realistic. In a (rare) moment of brilliance, I had an idea and just needed to coordinate a couple of things to make my plan work.

I spoke to my Marines about our communication and using all of the available resources (cameras and door alarms) to our advantage. I also told them that we were going to change things up and try something we hadn't before—whenever a new Marine arrived at the embassy, they would serve as the intruder within their first few days of being on the job. The idea being the new Marine would not be familiar with our tactics and could point out areas of improvement that we may be unaware of. Additionally, having the new Marine serve as the intruder was a perfect training opportunity for them to learn the floor plan of the embassy quickly. Rather than being unarmed, as previous intruders were, the new Marine would be armed, with eye protection and an airsoft pistol with plastic BBs. They would have the opportunity to shoot back. In addition, we were not going to carry our rifles but airsoft pistols as well, enabling us to shoot back. This change allowed us to simulate more of a realistic scenario than before. With a new Marine set to arrive in two weeks, I needed to ensure we had all of the new gear we needed.

With the new Marine on deck and reeling from jetlag, we ran the new-and-improved intruder drill. Once the two-minute head start passed, the Marines raced out to find the intruder with an intensity that I had not previously seen. "He is in the HR office," came over the radio as the Marine in the command center spotted the intruder on camera. The intruder was trapped, and the Marines and I were closing in. I screamed, "DROP YOUR WEAPON!" But the intruder did not comply. He instead raised his weapon with the intent to shoot, then the shooting started. The intruder began firing BBs at us and immediately caused the Marines to return fire. "OW! OW! OW!" followed quickly as we consistently hit the young Marine with the plastic BBs. Convinced the intruder was no longer a threat, I ended the drill and gathered everyone for the debrief.

Unlike other debriefs where we looked defeated, this debrief was filled with positive comments. There were no glaring gaps in our technique. The internal communication and better use of technology (our cameras and door sensors) enabled us to locate and trap the intruder quickly in an area that was advantageous to us. Our strategy and tactical movements were smooth, and the Marines were focused. Even with a two-minute head start, the intruder was no match for us. We were able to locate and subdue him in only three minutes. This was a significant improvement from the twenty to thirty minutes it had taken us to find Hema. The best part was, the Marines were eager and motivated to run the drill over and over again.

I didn't have to rethink my drills. No one told me I needed to change up the technique and simulate a real-word scenario. I acted in line with the Marine Corps definition of initiative: "taking action in the absence of orders." I just did it because I thought about the big picture—the Marines being well prepared and the embassy personnel being better protected in the event of an intruder. Yes, I benefited as well because my Marines believed and trusted in my leadership even more. But, that wasn't my motivation for making the adjustments.

In the business world, while we aren't necessarily ordered to do something, the essence of the definition of initiative is much the same. Initiative is about working independently and taking charge of a situation before others do. We often see terms and phrases like "self-starter," "proactive," and "grab the bull by the horns" either on job descriptions or performance reviews. These are all ways of saying that having initiative is important to the job.

Showing initiative looks like doing something before being told to do it. Seeing a problem and solving it before someone else does. Stepping in for a manager when they are out of the office. Proposing a process improvement to the executive team. There are countless other examples we see in the workplace every single day. But why is it so important in leadership?

Imagine being the lead on a large project that was about to go over budget. You have two options: you can either do nothing until your manager finds out or you can figure out a way to control the budget and manage costs differently. You need to talk to your manager, so you walk into their office to provide a project update. Your manager asks, "So tell me how we are looking on the budget?" What's your response?

If you went with the first response, do nothing, we're fairly certain your manager would immediately question how fit you were to serve as project lead. If you went with the second response and figured out a way to control the budget, you've demonstrated initiative, even if, in the end, you couldn't find a viable way to control the budget on your own. When talking to your manager, you would be able to explain the various paths you pursued to see if they would help save money. You didn't just walk into your manager's office with a problem, expecting them to solve it. You walked in with a problem and a potential solution before being prompted. Not only have you demonstrated initiative, but hopefully you've demonstrated good judgment, integrity, and dependability in the process.

The ability to show initiative strengthens relationships and shows others that you are eager and hungry for more responsibility. This is especially important when you are early in your career. Hema recently encountered a similar situation at one of our biotechnology start-up clients. Hema had been working with the CEO, CFO, and Board of Directors on creating a strong culture as the organization grew. One area she was focused on was pay. Everyone's pay was increased, some much less than others. After being told of his pay increase, which was minimal, one of the junior employees went to his manager's office, expressed sadness that his pay increase wasn't higher, and immediately followed it up with, "How can I increase my contributions to the organization, and what would it take for me to get promoted?" He was proactive in his approach, didn't expect anything handed to him, and was willing to work and gain experience to ensure he could get promoted. In turn, the manager reached out to Hema to discuss career path options and developmental opportunities for this junior employee. When the CFO found out about the employee's conversation, he said, "This is exactly the type of employee we want." Showing initiative gets you recognized, which in turn helps your career. Showing too much initiative, however, does have a dark side, which we will get to later.

We know initiative as a trait is important for everyone to possess. It's even more important when you're a leader. Others are watching you and learning from your example. If you make the first move, others will be more encouraged to follow.

How do You Show Initiative at Work?

We know initiative is important. But, how can you actually demonstrate it?

Remove the phrase, "But, this is how we've always done it," from your vocabulary. This phrase makes us cringe! We've all known someone at work, or maybe we've even been those people a time or two, who have uttered this phrase. If you do things how they've always been done, you'll continue getting the same results and won't stand out. Show initiative by getting creative and thinking about process improvements or ways you can make something better. As a leader, thinking outside of the box will encourage innovation in those around you. When this happens, ideas become better and you gain buy-in along the way (as it's a collaborative process). Your ideas are the best contribution you can make to your team, to your organization, and for your career.

Go above and beyond. You can look at your job description and talk to your manager about everything you *should* be doing in your current position. Consider those responsibilities the bare minimum of what you need to do. Chances are 85–90% of your organization is doing the bare minimum. They are good at their jobs and perform their duties adequately. There is absolutely nothing wrong with this. However, if you want to be recognized as a leader, you will need to do more. You will need to be exceptional to stand out. One way to do this is to focus on areas that may generate visibility and strong results. In one organization Hema worked for many years ago, a junior staff accountant in Finance couldn't understand why the printers were always out of paper and even the cabinets didn't contain extra reams. After asking around, she realized that she needed to adjust the printer settings on her computer to print double-sided. Otherwise, the printer would print on one side only, using double the amount of paper required. She talked to her manager and then to IT about the cost savings that could be recognized by changing the default printer settings on everyone's computer to print double-sided. IT agreed and made the update. After only a few months, the company recognized hundreds of thousands of dollars in savings as a result of this junior staff account. The CEO even recognized her at an all-employee meeting. The moral of the story? Taking initiative isn't just about your specific job. Think big and then take action.

Be open to all opportunities. New challenges and opportunities often appear when we least expect them. Keep an eye out and be prepared. If there is a new project starting and you're interested in it, raise your hand to be part of the team. Better yet, if you're qualified, ask to lead the project. When you ask for additional responsibilities or stretch assignments, chances are you will receive them. But if you don't ask, you will never know. Being open to new possibilities has trickle-down impacts. For example, you ask for more responsibilities, you're given more responsibilities, and you are successful. Your manager will be more likely to consider you for promotions or pay increases. Plus, you will inspire others around you as well.

Ask for feedback and take action. Think about a time when someone asked you, "Can I give you some feedback?" What was your initial reaction? How did you respond and what were you actually thinking? Likely, you may have responded with "sure" but were thinking "not really." When most of us hear this question, we do an internal eye roll. Why? Because we are preparing for the worst, or some type of criticism, and we're prepping our rebuttal. Leaders understand the best way to keep improving is to be proactive and ask for feedback. Don't just ask for feedback—act on it to improve in the future. After your next presentation, ask one or two people how you did and if they can provide you with some feedback that will help you next time. By being proactive and asking for someone's opinion, you do a few things. First, you are showing that you want to improve and are working on self-development. People are more apt to provide positive feedback in addition to areas of opportunity. Second, the other person feels like they have played a small role in your development. Lastly, they may be encouraged to ask for feedback next time as well, therefore helping create a culture where feedback is encouraged. The better one person does, the better the organization does. Everyone benefits. Once you have your feedback, think about it. Then incorporate it next time you have to do a presentation. Keep pushing the standard and creating a new, higher benchmark every time.

Lead with curiosity. One of the best ways to show initiative at work is to ask a lot of questions. Don't be shy. If you want to improve a process, policy, or procedure, it's important that you know how it works first. Be observant and thoughtful in your approach. Leading with curiosity isn't asking questions for the sake of asking questions. It's about gaining an understanding so you can think about it and analyze it to see if you can improve upon it. One great question to ask is, "Why have we always done it like this?" This question will provide you with insight into the original problem, which may no longer be applicable today. It also doesn't make people defensive. As we mentioned with tact, how you say something is just as important as what you say.

A technique that Hema has used in the past to better understand the root cause of a problem or situation is the "Five Whys" technique. This technique was originally developed by Sakishi Toyoda, whose son would later establish the automaker Toyota. The Five Whys was used within Toyota manufacturing. The technique is literally as easy as it sounds—this is an iterative process where you ask "Why?" five times, each question building on the previous answer. For example, you got a speeding ticket on the way to work.

1. Why? You woke up late.
2. Why? Your alarm didn't go off.
3. Why? The battery on your phone died.
4. Why? You didn't check if it was charged.
5. Why? You forgot to do it last night.

The root cause is generally the fifth why. In this example, had you checked your phone battery before bed, you would've known it was dying and would have charged it, ensuring your alarm went off. While a basic example, it's easy to see how the Five Whys technique can be used to get to the heart of the problem and perform a cause and effect analysis.

Be confident and get uncomfortable. Taking initiative is often about getting outside of your comfort zone and taking risks. In addition to being confident and asking questions, share your ideas. Be an active participant in discussions and speak up if you have an idea, especially if it's based in fact and/or experience. While it may feel uncomfortable to share and speak up at first, be self-assured and positive in your approach and keep doing it. It will get easier. This will also allow others, including your manager, to see how you think and process information. In the future, people will ask you for your thoughts and opinion in order to help them come to a decision. Actively offer solutions and ideas and be a problem-solver. But, be prepared to explain why you feel the way you do or why you are proposing a specific solution. The reasoning is very important, especially when building credibility.

Remain positive. This isn't always as easy as it sounds, especially during stressful times. But, complaining isn't helpful when you believe the process isn't as effective as it could be. Change can only be realized if you act. Rather than complaining, speak up about why you believe the process isn't effective and provide some solutions that can create an impact. Don't be discouraged if some of your ideas aren't implemented. The point is that you spoke up and provided justification for your solutions. Perhaps the final solution was even better than you could have imagined because it was a team effort, sparked by your confidence in offering alternatives. Remember others, including your manager, are watching.

It's easy to see how we can show initiative at work. But, as we mentioned, initiative does have a dark side.

The Dark Side of Initiative

Every leadership trait, much like every strength, has a dark side. When overused, or misused, it can actually be harmful to your reputation and your career. Initiative has the ability to be one of those traits. When you hear the phrase, "They came in, guns a blazing," who comes to mind? For us, we think of a new leader trying to prove themselves. In order to make change, they have to show initiative, so at the first team meeting, they start implementing new policies and altering processes. Employees are left wondering, "What just happened?" and thinking their new leader is going to be difficult to work for. While the intentions of the new leader may have come from a good place, the impact was less initiative and more dictatorship. The new leader didn't lead with questions in order to gain a better understanding before proposing changes. They led with answers and made changes rapidly. Yes, they took action and made adjustments, but they didn't necessarily demonstrate initiative, especially in front of their team.

Have you ever said the phrase, "It's easier/faster/quicker if I just do it myself?" We've certainly been guilty of this ourselves, especially early in our careers or when we had junior employees on the team. We *think* we're showing initiative by completing a task on our own. In reality, we are being poor leaders and not taking advantage of an opportunity to coach or teach someone else. We are also implying that we can do a better job than anyone else. While this may be the case with some things, the message being conveyed is one of arrogance and dismissiveness. Rather than doing it ourselves, if we took the time to show someone else how to do it, not only are we building a strong relationship with them, but they could find ways to improve upon the task or make a process better.

Doing it this way may take a bit longer to accomplish the task, but you will be showing initiative because you are mentoring the other person and teaching them along the way.

Another place we see initiative misused is something Mike calls "The Good Idea Fairy," similar to the "shiny new idea" people. These folks have lots of ideas, not always good ones. They are unable to focus on the present situation and what needs to get done. We all know at least one Good Idea Fairy. More often than not, their intentions aren't bad. They just lack the ability to be grounded in reality when necessary. Additionally, they can lack follow-through. The Good Idea Fairy can throw out ideas left and right and never actually execute or implement any of them before moving on to something new. While we've all been guilty of this at some point, it takes a conscientious effort to move to action while keeping those ideas in check and saving them for a more appropriate time. Initiative isn't coming up with new ideas for the sake of new ideas. Leaders need to strike a balance with being forward-looking and understanding present circumstances and priorities.

Good Idea Fairy Returns to Reality

I was sitting in my office, located under the flight deck, as the ship rocked back and forth, when my supervisor came in. He had a look on his face that I knew meant trouble. After exchanging pleasantries, he told me that he wanted to do a nine-mile department hike. I nearly spit out the water I was drinking. The thought of 150 Marines in full combat gear and heavy packs on our backs walking on a rocking ship sounded absurd to me. Among other things, someone was bound to go overboard, and I had no idea how we'd explain that to the Pentagon. I could tell he was serious, and as he furrowed his eyebrows, I knew that he didn't appreciate the smirk on my face. Gaining my composure and apologizing, I asked where the idea was stemming from and what his intent was.

As my supervisor explained his thoughts, I could not rebut any of his reasons. We were 120 days into our deployment, and our Marines were lethargic and needed a jolt to snap them out of it. I knew hikes were great for building mental and physical toughness. After hearing his rationale, I agreed that his idea, however off-the-wall, was worth a shot. It would also require a ton of coordination with the Navy and flight crew.

Three weeks later, we began our hike on the flight deck— 150 Marines split into two rows of 75. As the ship rocked and we walked in circles, I could not help but laugh. It was the crack of dawn, and we swayed and tried to keep our balance while walking. Due to flight operations, we were only allowed to be on the flight deck for an hour. Luckily, an hour wasn't long enough for nine miles! Plus, the flight deck surface was not conducive for long distance strolls while wearing eighty pounds of protective gear. Three miles later, as we completed our hike, my supervisor and I gathered the Marines and reminded them of Marines who fought in Korea and how they had to hike over twenty miles to reach the front lines. We put emphasis on why staying focused and keeping our bodies and minds sharp was so important. Based on their reactions, I knew the Marines understood what we were saying and that the point had resonated.

My supervisor's out-of-the-box idea, while positive in intent, had to be grounded in reality. His ability to not only come up with the idea, but to be flexible and work together to make it achievable and realistic, resulted in a successful hike and motivated Marines.

Putting It into Practice

Demonstrating initiative is a key leadership trait. Initiative isn't a quality but a behavior. Leaders demonstrate their initiative through their actions. Below are a few things you can start doing today to demonstrate initiative.

Learn something new. Have you been thinking about getting your Project Management Professional (PMP) certificate? Or are you considering signing up for a time-management class? Maybe you'd like to learn how to cook. Whatever it is, sign up for it! When you learn something new, you develop new skills which, in turn, builds your confidence. If you are interested in work training, talk with your manager or your Human Resources department about what you can do. Your organization may even offer a tuition-reimbursement program or training stipend, minimizing your out-of-pocket costs. Another way to learn something new is to volunteer for a new project, especially a stretch assignment. You will increase your knowledge and capabilities, thereby also increasing your comfort level with doing things outside of your comfort zone.

Practice the art of small talk. It's amazing how much you can learn through small talk. You probably work with many people who are outgoing and motivated. Maybe you've seen them volunteer for projects or ask for more responsibilities and thought, "I could never do that." Talk to these people and ask them for any advice they may have to help you on your leadership journey. In addition, you may learn something new in the way of job-related skills versus just interpersonal skills. The other person feels like they've helped you, and you gain insight from someone who has demonstrated initiative. Everybody wins.

Remove "I" and "me." Think "we." To really show initiative at work, you need to start thinking of the greater good and the larger collective. Stop thinking about yourself as an individual in a silo and start behaving as a member of a team. While taking initiative may benefit you personally (moving up in your career or showing your manager that you're hungry for more responsibilities), it does nothing for your leadership brand and reputation. If you focus on the success of the team and the organization, you will benefit just as much as your company. Plus, others will see you as a more of leader.

Taking initiative is necessary in both our professional and personal lives. It also tends to make leaders more accountable for their actions. By striking a balance between being ambitious and seeming overeager, leaders can show initiative and demonstrate their value.

CHAPTER 8

ENDURANCE

*The mental and physical stamina measured by the ability
to withstand pain, fatigue, stress, and hardship.*

As I side-shuffled to the bathroom, I looked directly into the drill instructor's office. I had two weeks left to graduate from boot camp, and I knew I wasn't supposed to look into the drill instructor's office. None of us were allowed to do this. But I forgot and did it anyway. Without fail, the drill instructor looked up, and we made direct eye contact. After a few moments of yelling (him at me), he wrote my name on the "kill list." The kill list is the equivalent of a teacher writing your name on the chalkboard when they catch you doing something wrong. After I left his office, I was immediately nervous. Once your name was on the kill list, you were on notice. Punishment was coming, you just didn't know when. I went to breakfast and tried to put it out of my mind. The morning came and went.

Then it happened. The drill instructor approached the front of the squad bay and yelled for everyone to get outside to march to lunch. Everyone but me. He didn't smile, but I could tell this was going to be fun for him and not so fun for me.

I was now running in place, my arms fully extended in front of me and knees coming up above my waistline. "Faster! Count louder!" I did what I was told. Next came push-ups. The drill instructor would say "up," and I would push up. Then he'd say "down," and I would lower myself, never allowing my torso to touch the ground.

Then it was back to running in place for a few minutes, then back to push-ups. After the fourth transition of push-ups, I was thoroughly drenched in sweat, but I was still going strong. I was going to finish with my head held high. It was mind over matter.

The icing on the cake was laying on my back and holding my legs six inches off the ground. After holding that position for about thirty seconds, the drill instructor removed his hat, what Marines call a "campaign cover." He proceeded to place it under my boots. I didn't need him to tell me why he was doing that. I knew that if my boots touched his campaign cover, the kill list would be the least of my issues.

I could feel every muscle and fiber in my legs and abdomen telling me to lower my legs. I could even feel them slowly falling. However, there was no way I was going to give up. Marines don't quit. This is what I was screaming in my head (well, that and some other colorful adjectives).

After what seemed like an hour, but was really under two minutes, my legs began to shake uncontrollably. Internally I was pleading with my body—just give me another ten seconds. To my relief, the door to the squad bay opened, and the drill instructor picked up his hat just before my legs gave way. Another drill instructor walked in and told me to hurry up and get downstairs with the rest of the platoon.

I had survived. My goal was to graduate from boot camp, and I was so close to achieving this. The kill list was definitely a roadblock, but I was determined to keep moving forward and not lose the progress that I had made to date. This was not just physical endurance, but mental endurance. A lesson in leadership focused on handling and overcoming obstacles. Two weeks later, I graduated boot camp.

This experience was a prime illustration of how the Marine Corps defines endurance: "The mental and physical stamina measured by the ability to withstand pain, fatigue, stress, and hardship." While the business world certainly comes with its fair share of fatigue, stress, and hardship, we hope pain doesn't enter the equation. From a business perspective, endurance isn't a word that comes up too often, mainly because when we think of endurance we think of *physical* endurance, like an athlete. Someone who can run for miles. However, from a mental perspective, endurance is key for leaders if they want to continue moving forward.

Leadership is an endurance sport. If you looked up the term *endurance sport* online, you would most likely see a definition encompassing submaximal activity for prolonged periods of time. This is leadership. You are always on, always needing to perform at your best, and always working toward a larger goal. Leadership is a marathon, not a sprint.

Leadership is also a growth journey. It comes with pain, struggles, self-doubt, and a whole host of other feelings and emotions. Endurance is what keeps leaders driving forward in spite of these doubts and fears. Leaders understand that overcoming these emotions will make them stronger, and they use these emotions to fuel their growth.

Why Does Endurance in Leadership Matter?

From a young age, we're taught that speed is important. How fast you run. How quickly you can get things done. We're rewarded for our quickness. But being quick doesn't matter as much as being able to endure, to continue for the long game. Take distance cycling. Lael Wilcox was the first American to win the Trans Am bike race, riding for 4,400 miles. On day eighteen, the final day of the race, she was trailing her competitor by forty miles. Rather than pushing herself the seventeen days prior and potentially injuring herself or tiring out, she pushed herself on the *final* day, finishing the race in first place. She knew the goal: to win. She had to pace herself to get there. Plus, she had to take the wins along the journey as well. This is how endurance works in business and leadership.

Endurance in leadership matters because leaders understand that when the team or organization does well, they benefit. They want to contribute to the overall vision and see things through. For leaders, the goal really is about making progress, getting closer to their destination. But a leader never reaches the final destination because a leader's job is never done. When one goal is met, the vision expands, and the goals get bigger and more complicated. More initiatives are added. More complexity is added. Each of the goals along the way is a milestone, but not the ultimate destination. And each achievement is considered a win, even if the end result isn't what they'd expected.

Take President Franklin Roosevelt's New Deal, his promise to recover from the Great Depression by putting money toward public works projects, financial reform, and other programs designed to help the US move forward. The Works Progress Administration (WPA) was part of the New Deal, and FDR needed $875 million to bring his vision to life. The House of Representatives reviewed his proposal and ultimately voted to only give him $725 million. While not exactly what he asked for, he took it as a win and still kept fighting for more. After a few months, he proposed the need for an additional $100 million, and the House granted it to him. In the end, because FDR persisted, he got 95% of what he asked for. He knew the long game.

Several years back, Hema encountered a similar situation, not for $875 million, but for promotions for two of her employees. She was proposing promotions for two of her direct reports. Both employees were qualified for the next level and had been performing exceptionally well in their current roles. However, the budget would only allow for one promotion. So Hema promoted the employee whose role was most critical to the organization based on the current corporate objectives. Three months later, she repitched the second promotion, making a case for why it was necessary in order to retain this employee. The promotion was approved. Had she given up and not pushed for the second promotion, the employee would have left, which would have been regrettable.

Endurance in leadership is also about recovery. How well a leader recovers from adversity or a setback is going to inform the next leg of their journey. Take the COVID-19 pandemic. Leaders needed to show a sustained effort as businesses started reopening. What were the organization's new strategies once reopened? What were the short- and long-term economic impacts of the pandemic on the organization? What about the operational and market challenges? On the surface, the goal appeared to be to *safely reopen*. However, that was a milestone in the larger picture, which was making the organization successful long-term.

The good news is you don't need to be an endurance athlete to show endurance as a leader.

How to Build Endurance in Leadership

Just like in sports, you do need to train and push the boundaries if you want to improve. In the case of business, and as a leader, you are responsible for not only yourself, but for your team as well.

Find your pace. Running marathons, cycling for 2,000 miles, or swimming long distances all require the right pace that allows the athlete to keep going and ultimately achieve their goal. Work is the same way. However, in the case of organizations, our pace is generally set by the pace of the organization. For example, start-ups move quickly, and the pace is relatively fast. On the other hand, more established (or mature) organizations may be steadier and more deliberate. Pace isn't constant, and it's a leader's job to understand when they need to speed up and when they need to slow down. Move too quickly and you run the risk of burnout (for yourself as well as for those around you), not to mention an increased likelihood of committing errors. Move too slowly and run the risk of your competitor going to market first or losing great talent because they had another job offer. To find your pace, consider the stage of your organization. Then think about the goals that you need to achieve. Do they require you to quicken your pace or slow it down? Just remember, faster is not always better. There's a saying we've used many times: "Sometimes you have to slow down to speed up." If you do something correctly and take your time setting the right circumstances for success at the onset, it will save you headaches and struggles in the long term, and you will be able to ultimately move faster.

Know your maximum threshold. This goes hand-in hand with finding your pace. Athletes push themselves right up to the point where any additional push could result in an injury. Business works the same way. In business, while there is the risk of physical harm if employees are pushed to their limits (i.e. a safety incident), there is also the risk of financial and reputational harm. All three—physical, financial, and reputational—reflect on a leader's ability to lead effectively or ineffectively. A well-known example of a brand learning their lesson the hard way was Samsung. When developing the Galaxy Note 7, Samsung was experiencing immense growth. They were competing with Apple and needed to outperform Apple and get to market faster. In doing so, they surpassed their maximum threshold, resulting in faulty batteries that were exploding on consumers. These phones were even banned on airplanes because of the danger. Samsung had to recall all phones, revisit the battery manufacturing process, and ultimately decided to discontinue the phone. When all was said and done, Samsung lost about $17 million in revenue, plus they paid additional damages to consumers. Samsung leadership was probably given a directive to get to market as soon as possible, in turn pushing their employees to speed up their pace, resulting in batteries not being assembled correctly.

Knowing your personal maximum threshold is a critical place to start. After how many hours do you need to take a break? How many days can you sustain working over eight hours without affecting your performance? We all need to take breaks, especially leaders who are playing the long game. Figure out your limits.

Have a clear plan with clear goals. Before embarking on any new project, ask yourself why you are on this journey to begin with. If you manage others, be sure to clearly articulate the "why" as well. This will also help you as a leader gain buy-in. Knowing and understanding the "why" will be helpful to keep moving forward. Don't lose sight of the vision. And if you find yourself asking, "Why are we doing this again?" think back to that vision and see if the path you are on still aligns. Having the big-picture vision and plan is great, but clear goals are necessary to make that vision a reality. For example, if your vision is to be healthy as you become older, a clear goal may be to lose fifteen pounds. This goal may have milestones along the way, such as losing five pounds each month for the next three months. Each month and each five pounds is a clear goal, a clear milestone marker along your bigger journey. The journey will have roadblocks, but endurance isn't about willing away these roadblocks. It's about leaders planning and mitigating the impact of the roadblocks. The planning and preparation are keys to success. Leadership endurance is about setting yourself up for success and giving yourself and the team the best circumstances possible to achieve success.

Practice Makes Perfect

"GO BACK AND DO IT AGAIN!" The late afternoon sun was beating down, and I was starving. My head was pounding, and my patience was wearing thin. I could see the look on my Marines' faces. They were exhausted and feeling the pressure to make the next dry run perfect. The goal was simple: the Marines had to walk together, stop, and salute on the appropriate cue. All things they had done before and

would do countless times in the future. Simple doesn't always mean easy.

It was a graduation ceremony. Not a presidential inauguration. A graduation ceremony that we had been rehearsing for multiple hours each day over the past week. I had anticipated going through two quick dry runs. I didn't expect that on day four, we would look as if we had never practiced before. Students were marching out of unison, turning the wrong way, some even saluting with the wrong hand (!!). These errors showed a lack of attention to detail, preparation, and discipline. But graduation was important. It was our chance to show battalion commanders and even generals all we had accomplished. We had to push through the fatigue and the mental and physical discomfort to perform the ceremony correctly.

After countless hours of practicing, it was finally game day—graduation, the final goal. I had just finished my pep talk with the students as the ceremonial music began playing. The music signaled the start of the ceremony. I looked around at the stands. They were packed with the families and friends of the students. The battalion commander and a two-star general were watching.

The large crowd and noise melted away as I issued and executed the ceremonial commands. With each order that was given, the Marines moved with crisp, flawless precision. They had pushed through the blisters on their feet, mental and physical fatigue, and other obstacles to reach the finish line and perform the ceremony perfectly.

It would have been easy for the Marines to give in to the stress or pain, but each one knew the goal and was committed to graduating with honor.

Be realistic. The best leaders can plan and prepare. But we all know the unexpected happens. As a leader, be realistic about obstacles. The business environment is dynamic and therefore constantly changing. The term VUCA (volatility, uncertainty, complexity, and ambiguity) has been used to describe such an environment. Initially used in a military setting, the term VUCA is now seen throughout business. There is only so much that is in our control. The COVID-19 pandemic is a prime example. Leaders didn't see it coming, and if they did, they didn't predict it would so dramatically upend work as we know it. Leaders who had established contingency plans may have been better prepared for the uncertainty. They were expecting that, at some point, a crisis would occur. On the other hand, leaders who didn't have a contingency plan, or were expecting an easy 2020, already started at a disadvantage. When this occurs, even the smallest challenge can seem like Mt. Everest.

Don't focus on only your strengths. It's easy to focus on our strengths and the areas we are great in. But, if I'm an endurance athlete who is strong at running and cycling yet struggles at swimming, how can I win a triathlon that requires excellence in all three? I look beyond my strengths and focus on what I need to win. In this case, I would need to focus on building my swimming capabilities. In business, this may look like talking with customers or clients to better understand how they use your product or service and taking their insights into consideration when determining how you can build additional capabilities or offerings. Maybe you are great at analysis, but are not a good public speaker, which is a critical skill for you to possess if you want to be promoted. Rather than playing up the fact that you are great at analysis, develop your public-speaking and presentation skills. Take a class or attend a seminar. This is also where initiative plays a role. Rather than assuming your strengths are enough, take the initiative to expand your capabilities in pursuit of the overall vision.

Get uncomfortable. Since we live in a VUCA world, having high, unwavering expectations may not be realistic, and staying within your comfort zone may be detrimental to your career. Hone your communication and change-management skills to really help people feel more comfortable with ambiguity. If you are responsible for a team, be sure to consider the audience and tailor the message as necessary. We all hear different things based on our filters. One important area we see that causes a great level of discomfort for leaders is the uncertainty around whether to communicate in the absence of having all the answers. In short, the answer is yes. While it can cause anxiety to give information without having all the answers, employees will appreciate the transparency and updates and it will allow them to keep moving forward, which is the goal. It's also okay to say you don't have all of the answers but wanted to share what you do have.

Look beyond competencies. Endurance is about the long haul, the resiliency to survive regardless of the circumstances. In business, the best way to do this is by focusing less on competencies and more on organizational capabilities. Another way to think about this is to fix the root cause and not just the symptoms. Let's say your organization routinely misses deadlines or is over budget on various critical projects. Saying employees should work more hours to achieve the deadlines or find cheaper solutions to come in under budget are ways of addressing the symptoms. But thinking about building-project management capabilities within your organization is a way of addressing the root cause of the problem, one central person to monitor and track progress of each department. As a leader, look beyond your world and take a look at the bigger picture. Are there capabilities, whether for yourself, your team, or your organization, that need to be considered if you want to succeed in the long term? If the answer is yes, then speak up.

Maintain momentum and motivation. You need momentum to keep moving forward. To gain momentum, you need to stay motivated and motivate those around you. Do not become complacent with your own leadership development. Remember, endurance in leadership isn't just about your organization. It's about you as a leader being able to go the distance. You need to keep learning new things, attending external events that broaden your knowledge and experience and that keep you motivated for achieving your ultimate goal. One word of caution. The more people look to you as a leader and rely on you to see projects and tasks through to the completion, the more recognition slips, and high-quality work becomes expected. It can be easy to lose motivation. This is where getting outside of your comfort zone is key to your own growth. To stay motivated, keep pushing yourself.

Leadership endurance is about combining strategy, communication, judgment, decisiveness, integrity, dependability, initiative, innovation, and optimism to keep propelling you forward. Endurance isn't about the final destination but the journey or the process to get there.

The Flow (State) of the Journey

Before we move on from endurance, we wanted to touch upon the idea of a "flow state." When we are fully immersed in an activity, we are energized, engaged, and motivated. This can often sound like "I'm in the groove" or "I've got good rhythm down" or even "I'm in the zone." These are all ways of saying you're in a flow state. When we're in a state of flow, we are focused on the process and concentrating on the tasks or projects that need to be completed. We tend to be focused on activities that bring us fulfillment and joy and that align well with our capabilities. As a result, we are more persistent and keep making forward progress.

In order to achieve flow at work, be sure you have clear goals, both at a corporate level and at an individual level. Know exactly what you need to accomplish and when. Also, give and receive feedback immediately. This allows you to make adjustments along the way. Finally, find a balance between doing more and maintaining a realistic capacity to do your best work. Flow states lead to personal growth and development and create happiness among employees. If all employees tried to achieve flow states within your organization, imagine what you could collectively create.

Think about the last time you felt like you were in a state of flow. What were the conditions that allowed you to achieve this? What were you doing? How long were you able to sustain the effort for? Then, think about how you can recreate those circumstances in the future to allow you to achieve flow more often. As a leader, talk to those around you about the concept of flow and help others find their own state of flow.

Putting It into Practice

Endurance isn't a trait that normally comes to mind when we think of leadership. But the ability to keep moving forward, and navigating setbacks and roadblocks in the process, is essential for leaders. Below are a few things you can start doing today to build your leadership endurance.

Conduct a "start, stop, continue" assessment. A "start, stop, continue" assessment allows you to look back on what's been done and whether any actions or behaviors need to be changed going forward. We've all heard the saying "Insanity is doing the same thing over and over and expecting a different result." When we don't get a different result, we get discouraged and are not able to effectively move forward. This "start, stop, continue" assessment goes over the items you need to begin doing (start), the items you should stop doing because they were ineffective and/or didn't serve your purpose (stop), and finally, the items that did work and that you should keep doing (continue). When a project is completed, whether an individual project or a team project, conduct this assessment. As you reflect on the project, think about when you were in a flow state and when you felt the most motivation and momentum. You can also use this assessment to look at your own leadership. Reflect on an area of your leadership. What do you need to start, stop, and continue doing? Focus on this specific area of your leadership to improve before moving on to a different aspect.

Build a support system. Leadership is a team sport. We all need a strong team to support us on our leadership journey. This can look different based on where you are on your own journey. For example, maybe consider a mentor or a coach. We've utilized both at various points in our lives. Mentors and coaches help us elevate who we are so we can contribute more and keep looking forward. Plus, they don't need to be formal mentors/coaches. These can be people whose leadership styles you admire in your current organization. Tell them about your journey and ask what proven methods, tips, etc. they may have for you. If you manage people, think about the team that is around you. You will need to have the right team to be successful. Don't be afraid to ask for help. Part of being a great leader is knowing your limits and tapping into others' strengths.

Schedule your day. Think about the time of day that gives you the most energy. Then schedule your most important activities for that time of day. If you have the most energy in the morning, use this time to work on the most valuable activities so you are more focused and at your peak. For us, mornings are when we are more effective and efficient at writing, when we're better rested. As the day goes on, it becomes harder for us to focus on writing. We use the afternoon to catch up on emails and other things that need to get done. Before leaving work for the day, make a list of everything you need to accomplish the next day. Use a calendar to actually schedule those items based on your energy level. When you return to the office, you are not only better prepared, but can get to work relatively quickly, allowing you to tap into your energy when it's high.

Much like physical endurance, leaders aren't necessarily born with mental endurance. We have to develop it, refine it, and create the circumstances that allow us to keep moving forward. Don't forget to celebrate the wins and accomplishments along the way. They serve as important motivators to keep going.

CHAPTER 9

BEARING

Creating a favorable impression in carriage, appearance,
and personal conduct at all times.

"**W**hy are you standing here again?"

An eruption was building inside of me as the young student standing in front of me began to speak. I was hoping he would admit his wrongdoing (that he was, indeed, smoking in the bathroom), I would give him a final warning, and we would both go our separate ways. However, this is not what happened. Instead, he responded with, "I didn't do anything wrong."

That was it. That eruption that was building was now on the surface and about to explode. My reaction could be heard throughout the building. Slamming my fists down on the table, I proceeded to inform the student that his conduct was unacceptable and would not be tolerated in the Marine Corps. Yes, he had been in my office for misconduct numerous times before, so we were familiar with one another. Yes, I had spoken to him about the importance of following the rules and instructions at all times. Yes, this was a clear pattern of bad judgment and behavior on his part.

But, the offense didn't warrant the level of my response. All I saw was red.

I should have stopped myself, but I kept screaming at the student, getting more personal in my tactless verbal assault. It was only once I saw tears in his eyes that I finally stopped and sent the student away. I'd lost it. Pure and simple. My emotions had taken over.

Earlier in the day, I found out that I wasn't getting promoted. My dream of following in my mentor's footsteps was not meant to be, and I didn't know how to feel about it. I would not be promoted to the highest enlisted rank. In not being selected for promotion, I had to wait another year and hope to be promoted then. Another failure would mean I would be forced to retire. For months, my peers and superiors alike had told me that I was guaranteed a promotion. Unfortunately, in the Marine Corps, they aren't the ones who make the final decision.

Not getting promoted was all I could think about. I was angry, sad, and, most of all, in shock. I was consumed by my emotions and thoughts when that poor student knocked on my door.

I had lost all semblance of being a leader. At that moment, I was a tyrant. The department leader sitting next to me was stunned. He had witnessed the whole scene and had never seen me lose my composure like that before. To be honest, in my nearly twenty-three years in the Marine Corps, I had never lost my composure like that before.

My superiors emerged from their offices to see what the commotion was. My boss calmly motioned me into his office and asked me to take the rest of the day off. It was clear to everyone that I was going to do more harm than good if I stayed at work. My demeanor and body language illustrated what I was feeling, and I clearly could not control my temper and emotions that day.

The Marine Corps defines bearing as, "creating a favorable impression in carriage, appearance, and personal conduct at all times." Clearly, I lost my ability to do any of these things upon hearing the negative news about my promotion. The business world defines "bearing" in much the same way. In fact, we would even use the phrase "leadership presence" to describe how a leader carries themselves, not just in appearance but in the words and phrases they use, in their tone, and in their overall demeanor.

In the business world, much like in the Marine Corps, leaders are given a reprieve if they lose their bearing once or twice, especially when it's completely out of character for them. Luckily, this was the case with Mike. However, leaders who routinely lose their bearing also lose their ability to effectively lead.

Often, especially early in our careers, we think that being a leader is about more responsibility and making the tough decisions. We think leaders have authoritative body language and calculated speeches and intonations, and therefore, we think by mimicking these stylistic nuances, we, too, can become a leader. People can see through this act. The problem is we overlook the importance of how we handle situations. We think that bulldozing and clawing our way to the top is the way to go. This couldn't be further from the truth. Think about the truly effective leaders that you have either had or seen in your career. What did they have in common? They probably were articulate, behaved in a manner that was aligned with their values, as well as the values of the organization, and related to people in a way that helped them showcase their true impact. They were authentic.

As Mike's story demonstrated, we all have the ability to lose our bearing at one point or another. While minimizing these instances is important, recognizing and overcoming missteps is equally as important. The good news is, leadership presence can be developed. It's all about how you carry yourself as a leader. After all, if you want to be a leader, you have to play the part first.

How to Carry Yourself as a Leader

If you want to be recognized as a comedian, you need to be funny and be comfortable on a stage. If you want to be a famous artist, you need to enter your art in showings. If you want to be a leader, you need to walk the walk and talk the talk. So, what exactly does this mean? It means even if you aren't recognized as a leader today, whether you manage people or not, there are behaviors, thoughts, and actions that you can incorporate into your daily life to develop the leadership mindset. Remember, leadership isn't a role or a title. It's an attitude.

Be organized. What does your desk look like at work? Are there papers piled up everywhere? Do you have old, dirty coffee cups sitting around? How many personal items are on display? It may sound funny, but your desk or office says a lot about you and your leadership style. Others may be more confident in your abilities if they see a neater desk. That doesn't mean that you can't have papers or files out, especially if you are using them. It does mean that items should be easy to find on your desk. Time can often get away from us in the middle of the day. While we may have the best intentions to tackle the pile of paperwork, sometimes it just doesn't happen. Hema would designate a cabinet in her office where she would put these items so her desk remained clean. She wouldn't forget about them because there would be a note on her desk reminding her that she needed to go through the pile. However, the pile wasn't visible for all to see.

Use assertive—not aggressive—language. "Perhaps we should…" "I have a stupid question." "This may be a dumb idea, but…" Do any of these phrases sound familiar? We've all used them at some point in our careers. Replace these phrases with, "In my opinion…" "I have a different opinion. I feel that…" "One idea I have is…" Assertive language is not passive and it's not aggressive. It is direct and honest and based in confidence. There's a fine line between being assertive and being aggressive. Assertiveness is about standing up for yourself in a respectful way. Aggression is about threatening, attacking, or ignoring others. Using assertive language is all about communication style.

Watch your nonverbal cues. Your body language speaks volumes, even when you're silent. These nonverbal cues not only help boost confidence but they send the right message to those around you, boosting your leadership presence. First, make eye contact. Don't stare at your shoes when talking to someone. Instead, look them in the eyes. If you're in a room full of people, look around the room as you speak. But, don't stare. This can get awkward. Also, start smiling! A smile is a sign of approachability and confidence. Think about a coworker who hardly smiles. Can you easily tell what they are thinking? How comfortable do you feel approaching them when you have a question? Chances are you avoid them. This is not part of leadership presence. Finally, maintain a strong posture. Sit or stand up straight. Try not to cross your arms when talking to others, which can be viewed as an aggressive gesture. And if you don't know what to do with your hands, put them down by your sides. Your body language and these nonverbal cues are a great place to start practicing leadership presence and gain confidence.

Splinters

Boom! "DOWN!" Crack! "UP!" The drill instructor was in rare form as he screamed and pounded on the old podium with a wooden dowel. He was punishing the squad leaders for a particular reason, known only to him, while the rest of us cleaned our weapons. I had a near front-row seat to the action. I was about fifteen feet away, and I could see the spit from the drill instructor's mouth flying in all directions as he yelled at the squad leaders doing push-ups and other exercises. We all knew better than to look up and watch the drill instructor, but it was incredibly hard not to watch what he was doing and even harder not to laugh. Any recruits caught laughing joined the drill instructor's push-up party. With each obscenity the drill instructor yelled, he seemed to catch another recruit losing their bearing and laughing hysterically. Of course, the laughing ceased immediately when the recruit's eyes locked with the drill instructor's.

Recruit after recruit was caught, punished, and sent back to continue cleaning their rifle. The drill instructor kept a steady group of ten at his push-up and exercise party. With every command, the drill instructor would bang his wooden dowel on the podium. I began to notice the podium was coming apart and splintering into small pieces. Each time, I would sneak a peek to look at the drill instructor, the podium was getting smaller and smaller, and the pile of splinters on the floor was getting taller and taller.

After nearly two hours of steady screaming and banging, the drill instructor hit the podium one last time before it came crashing down and fully fell apart. With nothing left to hit, the push-up and exercise party was officially over. I looked up one last time and caught the drill instructor admiring his handy work. I caught the slightest smirk on his face and a faint chuckle. Drill instructors don't laugh in front of recruits. They maintain their rough and serious demeanor at all times. From my recruit perspective, the drill instructor was still the model Marine. However, if another drill instructor would have seen his reaction, it would have been seen as negative or unprofessional. This drill instructor had lost his bearing. He quickly realized what he was doing and regained his composure before he started screaming at us again.

Watch your words. We are not talking about assertive or aggressive language here. We are talking about outright rude language, such as the use of profanity. Yes, we all get mad, and a word or two may slip out every now and then. As a leader, part of maintaining your composure and keeping your bearing is not to lose your cool, especially in front of your direct reports and in public settings. While this may be more acceptable in the military world, in the business world, it definitely speaks to someone's ability to lead effectively. The candor should be saved for private conversations, perhaps amongst peers.

There are also non-profane words that should be kept out of your vocabulary. For example, the word "just." Leaders tend to use "just" to soften their approach when asking others to do something, "I just need you to do three small tasks for me." What you think you're communicating is that you don't want to impose on the other person. What is being heard is these are small, insignificant things that you don't want to do. Instead of using the word "just" in our example, another way to phrase it would be, "This task isn't big, but it is essential." Another word to use is "because." *Because* is an easy way to gain credibility. It provides a reason for your actions. It allows you to be truthful and diplomatic while being succinct and decisive.

Clothes make the man or woman. You may think it doesn't matter what you wear. That people aren't judging your abilities based on how you dress. The truth is, yes they are. While this may look different in our remote/virtual work world thanks to COVID-19, our appearance still serves as a visual cue for people. We're not saying you have to wear a business suit, but do make sure your clothes are cleaned and ironed, especially if you are seeing other people. For example, in our remote environment, on days where we do not have video calls with clients, we are generally in clean and comfortable clothing (a.k.a. workout clothes). However, when we meet with clients and prospects, we put more effort into our appearance and wear something more appropriate for the situation.

A casual dress code is more and more common in office settings, and we're huge fans of this. However, the problem that we've seen is that people take the term "casual" a bit too far. In one organization Hema worked for, a leader in the Product Development department, in addition to wearing jeans with holes in them, wore a T-shirt that said, "I Can't Adult Today." Forget the fact that the organization provided clear guidelines to all employees on what a casual dress code actually meant, complete with pictures of what to do and what not to do. As a leader, he should have known better. His team took their cues from him. His clothing choices communicated that it was okay to dress in such a manner.

Be goal oriented. Think of goal setting on a micro and macro level. On a macro level, set overarching personal and professional goals for yourself. Also, consider your individual goals that you have set within your organization. Having goals is another way of being organized. Goals allow you to prioritize what is most important. In addition, having clear goals helps leaders communicate their vision in a simple way, ensuring alignment and buy-in along the way. Display your goals for others to see. They will see you are focused. On a micro level, think about your day. If you're attending a networking event, for example, set a goal to find at least one way to help every person that you connect with. By moving the focus away from yourself and onto the other person, you will connect differently and build your leadership presence in the process.

Be humble and respectful. We can't stress enough how important these two qualities truly are in leadership. As we've mentioned, business and leadership are team sports. As a leader, you may be accountable for the final product or end result, but no single person deserves the credit for the success of the whole. If you are a member of a team, be sure to give credit where credit is due. Thank your team members for all coming together to achieve the goal. If you manage others, be sure to recognize those who positively contributed to the final success. Saying thank you is free, but the goodwill, positivity, and engagement it can create is priceless. Being respectful should go without saying. However, there is a reason we are mentioning it. All too often, leaders forget this. Respect the work of the team and the contributions of everyone. This goes hand in hand with saying thank you. Some of the least effective and least liked leaders we have come across are far from humble. They not only want sole credit, but they also have an air of arrogance and overconfidence, resulting in others avoiding them at all costs.

Putting It into Practice

While commonly referred to as "leadership presence" in the business world, bearing is essential to our leadership brand and reputation. How we carry ourselves in both stressful and non-stressful times determines how others see us. With regards to bearing and carrying yourself as a leader, think of the saying *fake it till you make it*. The more you act like a leader, both in what you say and in your body language, the easier it will become. Below are a few things you can start doing today.

Be aware of your actions and behaviors. When you're talking to your manager or speaking in front of a crowd, are you aware of your hand gestures or the words you are using? Do you say "um" a lot or use other filler words? Do you use a lot of hand gestures because you don't know what to do with your hands? Before a presentation, record yourself or practice in front of a mirror. Notice whether you're making eye contact or looking at your slides the whole time. Pay attention to the tone of your voice and speed of your speech. Do they convey confidence or fear? If you're talking about a subject that you are passionate about, could your passion come across as aggression to others?

In addition, try to increase your awareness of your everyday attitudes, thoughts, and intent. You need to be aware of how you are behaving when you believe no one else is watching. Pay attention to your facial behaviors when various thoughts come into your head. Most of all, try not to judge yourself. Be compassionate with yourself and simply observe. Your goal in observing yourself, whether during the day or on video, is to look at how you are showing up. Are you active or passive? Strong or weak? Try and think about what kind of person you look like to yourself. Based on what you're observing, would you consider yourself a leader? Once you are aware, you need to decide what to do about it. But gaining awareness is the first and most important part.

Ask someone about your behaviors. It can be difficult to be objective and non-judgmental about our own actions. After all, we are our own harshest critics. If you are finding it difficult to be truly objective about yourself, then ask close friends, family, or even colleagues for some help. Rather than asking someone to follow you around all day, ask them to rate you on a scale of one to ten on factors such as charisma, leadership, confidence, vocabulary, and presence. In addition, you can ask them targeted questions such as: "How upbeat would you say I am normally?" or "How easy is it for you to tell when I disagree with another?" These questions are rated on a scale of one to ten again, making them easier for others to answer versus open-ended questions. When asking your trusted group, you aren't analyzing individual answers because each will see different sides of you depending on your relationship. Instead, look for patterns. If you are already a leader, one way to gauge how you show up is through 360 evaluations, where you ask colleagues, peers, and even your manager for feedback. People are normally very good at reading the emotional attitudes of people they know well and interact with often. For example, we know when our coworker is in a good mood or having a difficult morning. Again, it's important to not look at individual comments but at patterns around your usual mood, attitude, behaviors, etc. Those patterns will also tell you about your physical presence.

Use the word "but" very carefully. "Thanks for the idea, but…" "Your performance was good, but…" We tend to brace ourselves when we hear the word *but* following anything positive. In fact, using but can quickly negate anything positive that was said before it. If you intend to be positive, remove "but." When leaders use this word, they can come across as insincere and unappreciative. For example, instead of saying, "Thank you for the feedback, but I think my way is still best," try, "I've considered your feedback, and I still believe in the decision I've made." By using the word "and," you are communicating that you have considered someone else's point of view or opinion before making a decision. You aren't dismissing them. When you are observing yourself, count how many times you say "but." Then, try to replace it with words like "and" or "because."

Stop saying "I'm so busy." News flash, everyone is busy! Constantly telling other people how busy you are will make them wonder how effective you truly are. Leaders understand that they need to effectively prioritize their life and say no to things that take them away from what they are focused on and trying to accomplish. When someone asks, "How have you been?" do not answer that you've been busy. Instead, stay positive and perhaps mention an item that you have been focused on. For example, "I've been really good, focusing on a new project at work and learning a lot." In addition to remaining positive, you've communicated that you are taking on more responsibilities and enjoy what you do. This will open the door to further conversation.

Showing up as a leader and carrying yourself in a manner that makes you recognizable is beneficial for you both personally and professionally. However, do not confuse confidence with competence. Maintaining your composure and your bearing during stressful and non-stressful times is only part of being a leader. You still have to know what you are doing.

CHAPTER 10

UNSELFISHNESS

*Avoidance of providing for one's own comfort and
personal advancement at the expense of others.*

I was in the operations tent, getting ready to check on the Marines, when I saw my operations director walk by carrying a three-gallon coffee container. He was slipping and sliding in the mud, making his way ever so slowly to a group of Marines. When he made it to the first group of Marines, he pulled out a stack of paper coffee cups from inside his jacket and started to pour hot coffee for everyone. The Marines were thrilled. It was as if Santa had visited. Each Marine wore an ear-to-ear grin and thanked the operations director profusely.

We were already about halfway through a two-week exercise in the middle of Camp Pendleton. The weather was wet, cold, and absolutely miserable. The weather also made our training increasingly difficult and dangerous—there is nothing safe about carrying, loading, and shooting one-hundred-pound artillery shells in the middle of a downpour. As rain continued to drench the Marines, the morale began to decline. With very little reprieve from the elements and no real way to get warm and dry, we could only hope for a break in the weather.

After my operations director passed coffee to half of the Marines, I watched him do something even more remarkable. He spotted a Marine that forgot to bring his wet-weather gear. Without any judgment or hesitation, the operations director offered his own jacket to the young man. Then he continued passing out coffee to the rest of the Marines, all while getting soaked. He was not focused on being cold or wet, or sliding and nearly falling in the mud. He was focused on each of the subordinate Marines and bringing them some comfort to boost their morale.

Fast forward two months, and this same operations director had just finished working a twenty-four-hour shift when I saw him walk into the office. It was seven in the morning. I knew he was exhausted, so I told him to go home and get some sleep. The operations director said he was just going to check his email, and then he would leave. Then I watched and listened to Marine after Marine ask him for a moment of his time. Never once did he say no or that he was tired. Seeing a chance to help, he seized every opportunity. Some Marines asked for advice for a personal situation that they were dealing with. Others asked technical questions regarding a weapon system. With every interaction, my operations director was engaged and present and not worried about himself. I went on with my day thinking he would eventually go home.

It was early evening when I walked out of my office, and the operations director was still there. A senior leader was putting together a training session for his Marines and was having difficulty developing a detailed curriculum. The operations director was getting ready to leave when he asked the senior leader if he needed any help. Understanding that he needed expert assistance, the senior leader was about to say yes, but when he saw the bloodshot eyes of the operations director, he attempted to say no. However, the operations director was already sitting down, ready to help. For the next three hours, they worked together to develop a comprehensive training session. In the process, the operations director also taught the senior leader an easy method that could be used to put together future training sessions.

The operations director worked well over thirty-six straight hours. Yes, he was tired, and yes, he wanted to go home and see his family. But his ability to put the needs of others before his own was remarkable. His patience, demeanor, and willingness to help never faltered. His selfless leadership approach had a great impact on the collective unit and inspired all of the Marines he encountered.

When performance-review time came around, these examples of selflessness and true leadership came to mind. In fact, this operations director was one of the most unselfish leaders that I had served with in nearly 23 years. I could not think of a time where he put his needs above others. If a Marine needed his help, he was there, no questions asked. He not only left a lasting impact on his Marines, he made all of us want to be better by being around him.

This operations director truly embodied the Marine Corps definition of unselfishness: "avoidance of providing for one's own comfort and personal advancement at the expense of others." In the business world, we would define it in much the same way. However, we may use terms such as "selfless leadership" or "servant leadership" versus "unselfishness." We've all had leaders who were more focused on their title and the potential power they wielded. When someone questions their authority or gets in their way, they are on a one-way ticket out of the organization. It becomes easier to appease them versus standing up to them. Sometimes, the worst part is they may be good at their job and able to make the company money. But everyone sees them as selfish, even though they can't see it for themselves. It's easy to see through their facade, what they call "leadership." We also need to remember that it's easy for others to see through our facade as well. People can tell when we are being disingenuous. So often, we only focus on ourselves and lose sight of the fact that we need to serve those we lead as well as those we work with.

The Marine Corps is built on teamwork. They don't have the luxury of being selfish, at least not in many combat and training scenarios. In business, we see selfishness in leadership displayed in both large and small, public and private organizations. This can occur because people easily confuse being a true leader with things like power, authority, aggression, and winning. In reality, being unselfish is a sign of strength. It's easy to only focus on ourselves. But focusing on other people takes dedication and commitment. It takes focus and intentionality. So why is being unselfish or being a servant leader so important?

Being selfless displays your confidence in your competence. Selfishness in leaders generally comes from a place of fear that their incompetence may be found out. By focusing on others and on the greater good of the team or organization, you are demonstrating that you are knowledgeable in your area and are not threatened by others who may have more knowledge than you.

Being selfless shows your commitment to others, whether you manage them or not. A servant leader is focused on growth, both their own as well as that of other people. When everyone feels valued and is developing, the team and organization benefit. Selfless leaders encourage others to pursue their ideas and to think for themselves. At their core, servant leaders are teachers and not micromanagers.

Being selfless maximizes the talent of others. Servant leaders understand they are not always the smartest person in the room. They are not threatened by hiring or working with people who may be smarter than them because they realize that the collective knowledge will only benefit the team.

There are countless reasons why being unselfish as a leader is important. The truth is, being a servant leader is not only beneficial to a team, organization, or any other relationships in your life, but it also feels good. When you help others, you benefit as well. Being a selfless leader is a mindset shift. It's easy for us to think about the quickest and fastest way to gain power, make money, or move up in our organizations. So how can you become more selfless?

Elements of an Unselfish Leader

It's easy for us to describe selfish leaders. They are self-centered. They only care about how something benefits them personally. They criticize others behind their backs. They are risk averse. However, everyone can become a selfless leader. Here's how.

Share the credit. Unselfish leaders do not hoard all of the credit for themselves. They recognize the achievements and successes of others, whether those people played a starring role in the project or were more in the background. As we mentioned before, servant leaders are not threatened by others who may be smarter than them or work harder than them on a task or project. A selfless leader understands that by sharing the credit, their leadership is on display, and they, too, are being recognized for a job well done.

Initiate the conversation. An unselfish leader engages in open and honest dialogue. They ask for feedback and listen to it with an open mind. They engage in dialogue because they know that in the absence of information, people will make up their own stories. Selfless leaders will ask, "What could I have done differently on that project that could have been more beneficial to you/the team?" They understand conversation is a two-way street and do not try to control the message or steer the narrative, like a selfish leader often does.

Bring others on the journey. Selfless leaders know they can't do it alone. They tap into the strengths of others to achieve the final outcome. They understand that in so doing, they not only help themselves, but help others along the way too. A number of years back, Hema worked for an organization where she was hired to help build the HR infrastructure and build and grow the HR team. Early on, there were three leaders on the HR team, of which Hema was one. All three needed to work together to bring the vision to life. In addition, each leader had to grow their own teams and hire people who had strengths, which were different from their own. It was the only way to build an infrastructure that scaled a two-hundred-employee company into a nearly seven-hundred-employee company in eighteen months. The three were successful in their mission, and as the organization grew, the team members hired were promoted and moved up as well.

Conceptualize and execute. Servant leaders can conceptualize the future. They can see the possibilities and what can be. However, they reconcile this with current circumstances and reality. They bridge the gap between what can be and what is and work to bring everyone together to make the vision a reality.

Be present and listen. In leadership positions, it can be easy to want to go into problem-solving mode. The truth is, not every problem is yours to solve. Sometimes people just need a sounding board. They just want someone to be present, to listen without judgment. Leaders can often feel that when they jump in to help solve the problem, they are showing their leadership capabilities. The truth is, they are showing their power. A truly selfless leader will ask questions to help the other person solve their own problem.

Give unconditionally. Selfless leaders give without expecting anything in return. In the business world, this is more about giving time versus money. For example, if there is a new member of your team, take them on a tour of your office and introduce them to others. This doesn't cost you anything, and you are building a relationship with a new member of the team. It's a win-win.

When No One is Looking

A young, eighteen-year-old man sat down. He was being interviewed by a Marine liaison to determine whether he would be accepted into the Marine Corps. The young man was disheveled—his T-shirt was dirty, his workout shorts had worn thin, and his athletic shoes were falling apart. He didn't look like most of the other people who sat down for an interview. Most others at this stage walked in wearing a collared shirt, slacks, and dress shoes. After looking at the young man's file, it was clear to the Marine liaison that the young man was homeless, and there might be complications in qualifying him to serve in the Marine Corps. Due to the intense pressure to send only qualified applicants, Marine liaisons disqualify applicants for even minor discrepancies, like not wearing the appropriate attire. But this Marine liaison was not like many others in his position. He looked beyond skin color, race, and attire and saw a person who wanted to serve his country. The young man's circumstances were less than fortunate, but the Marine liaison could help change that.

The Marine liaison asked the young man why he wanted to join the Marine Corps. After reviewing his file, the Marine told the young man that he could not sign off on his enlistment, his contract to join the Marine Corps. The young man was not qualified because he was missing critical documentation. Then the Marine liaison gave him a detailed list of documents he was missing. He also contacted a local Marine recruiter to help the young man get most of the documents. The Marine liaison stood up, shook the young man's hand, and told him that he expected to see him again, and that if he needed any assistance, to call him directly. It had been a long time since the young man had felt heard or received respect from an adult. He felt a renewed confidence and determination as he shook the Marine liaison's hand.

A week later, the young man once again sat at the Marine liaison's desk. He had tracked down all of the missing documents and was ready to go to boot camp. The Marine liaison reviewed the documents and completed the remaining paperwork. With everything complete, the Marine liaison reached under his desk for a box and handed it to the young man. Looking confused, the young man took the box and opened it. It was a new pair of athletic shoes, a necessary staple when entering boot camp.

The young man was overcome by the selfless and kind gesture. He profusely thanked the Marine liaison. The Marine liaison's last words to the young man were to come back and see him after he graduated boot camp. The Marine liaison changed the young man's life through a series of unselfish and kind gestures. He showed genuine care and concern for another human being.
—*Story as told by Captain Michael Krueger, United States Marine Corps.*

Care equally. A selfless leader looks past skin color, race, religion, language, etc. They care about everyone equally, and they don't pick and choose who to help or who to serve. They are also transparent with everyone, as they understand the team is really the sum of its parts.

Selfless leadership is about looking beyond how something can benefit you personally and thinking about how it can benefit the greater good. It's about putting your ego aside and, as we mentioned with integrity, it's about doing what's right for the collective, even if it may not be right for you. But how can you tell if you're being selfish or selfless?

Are You Being Selfish or Selfless?

Much like other aspects of leadership, being selfless can take a conscientious effort, especially at the beginning as you rewire your brain to be more selfless. Here are some questions to ask yourself to determine just how selfless you are being in any given situation.

Do you seek out opportunities or take the initiative to serve others? We're not talking about delegation here. We're talking about perpetually providing support and guidance to others.

When someone interrupts you, how do you respond? When you're viewed as a leader, you can see an increase in "drive-bys," people stopping by to ask a question, seek advice, etc. Think about Mike's operations director. He was ready to help every time he was interrupted. Your response to these interruptions is important because even the smallest sign of frustration or annoyance will drive people away. If you're in the middle of something important, consider saying, "I'd love to help. I am in the middle of this project and need to finish my thought process. Can I come see you in ten minutes?"

How do you use your words? Selfless leaders use their words to encourage others. Selfish leaders use their words to criticize others, especially in an attempt to make themselves look better.

How much time do you spend trying to protect your domain? It's nearly impossible to be a selfless leader if you are only focused on your work, your department, or your resources.

Do you take advantage of your position for personal gain? Selfish leaders use their position or power to get ahead personally while holding others down. Selfless leaders do not.

It seems relatively easy to spot a leader who is unselfish. However, before we move on, we want to make one note about being selfish versus taking care of your own health.

Selfishness vs. Self-Care

Hema has found herself in countless conversations with leaders who struggle with not wanting to be viewed as selfish but who are in need of a break and need to take time for self-care. It's important to remember that we're not talking about putting your health or wellness at risk when we talk about being unselfish. This isn't about working too many hours to help others or taking on more than you can manage because you want to be viewed as a team player.

Self-care should not be mistaken for being selfish. If you want to continue performing at a high level, moving up in your career as a leader and making an impact, taking time for yourself is important. When a leader is selfish, they take from other people and behave in a manner that is self-serving. When a leader takes time for themselves to recharge, they are not depleting resources from someone else. They are refueling their tank so they can continue to serve others and keep their personal energy high.

For many years, we both thought that working sixty plus hours a week, accepting more and more responsibilities, and never saying no were all signs that we were team players and high performing. While they may have been signs we were team players, we were by no means high performing at all times. We neglected health for longer work hours and exchanged time away to recharge to take on new projects. It wasn't until a decade or so ago that we realized work will always be there, but our health will not. And if we truly wanted to be great leaders for our teams, we needed to focus on our wellbeing.

Putting It into Practice

Unselfishness or selflessness are words that we often associate with true leadership. We think of leaders like Nelson Mandela, Abraham Lincoln, and Rosa Parks. These leaders who put the interests of others first because they knew that when everyone succeeded, they would too. You don't have to impact world history in order to be a selfless leader. You just need to impact those immediately around you. Below are a few things you can start doing today to become a selfless leader.

Test your motives. Before doing something, ask yourself why. When faced with a decision, our first instinct can easily be to ask, "What's in it for me?" This is commonly referred to as WIIFM. Rather than focusing solely on yourself, broaden your lens. What will the impact of your decision be on others? The next time you need to set individual objectives at work, think about why you are setting those particular objectives. Is it solely to get promoted or is it in the best interests of your team and organization?

Keep your emotions in check. When you don't like a decision that's been made, how do you react? Do you criticize others behind their backs? Do you throw a tantrum and emotionally protest? Selfless leaders understand that these loud and obvious displays of emotions are selfish. They hurt your leadership brand and reputation, and they hurt the morale and engagement of those around you. Next time you don't agree with a decision or have a differing opinion, don't respond immediately. Think about how the decision that was made affects everyone and if it was in the best interest of the majority. If you are still unsure, ask to speak with the person who made the decision. Be respectful in your interaction and lead from a place of inquiry and seeking to understand.

Be kind. It can be easy for leaders to think that kindness doesn't have a place in business and that being kind is a sign of weakness. This couldn't be further from the truth. Kindness is about treating people like people and not as resources or means to an end. Selfish leaders treat others as pawns to use to their benefit in achieving success, recognition, etc. Selfless leaders celebrate other people's successes, give others the benefit of the doubt, and create an environment of trust. Before speaking, think about the impact of your words and try to stay positive. Start small by complimenting one person every day. Work up from there.

A strong leader thinks more about others than about themselves. They are always trying to find ways to assist their team, remove obstacles, and develop others. But even unselfish leaders need time to replenish their energy and focus on their health. Be sure you are striking a balance between being a servant leader and caring for yourself. Both are critical to being a high-performing leader.

CHAPTER 11

COURAGE

Courage is a mental quality that recognizes fear of danger or criticism, but enables a Marine to proceed in the face of danger with calmness and firmness.

"Hey, sir, can I talk to you for a few minutes?"

I needed to have a difficult conversation with my boss. I didn't want to do it, but I needed to do it. This was the third time in as many days that my boss had made a decision or said something that negatively impacted my unit. As I walked into his office, I could feel the nerves and butterflies growing in my stomach. My boss was extremely intelligent and headstrong, but his strength was not in emotional intelligence or communication. I needed to tell him that he was derailing his own unit.

With my notes in hand, I walked into his office and sat down. It was the end of the day, so I knew we wouldn't be interrupted. I sat there nervously thinking about how I was going to say what needed to be said. "How do you think the unit is performing?" I asked. I knew he was going to be highly critical of the leadership, and he was. He said that he was very frustrated by the executives and department leaders. In his opinion they lacked drive and were unable to accomplish simple tasks to his standards.

This was my opportunity to move the conversation in a different direction. I asked him how he and I could work together to improve the performance of our leadership team. My goal was to find an opening to talk to him about his leadership style and hopefully get him to realize the effects of his actions. Before he could answer, I followed up my question with my own observation of the Marines' performance and how the collective morale was declining. I could see the look on his face change, and I could feel the tension increasing exponentially. The mood in the room had changed too—I was indirectly implying that the leaders' poor performance could be the result of his, and my, actions.

"I don't care about their morale. That will improve when they do their jobs better." I was floored and had to pause before responding. I collected my thoughts and tempered my irritation. With my blood pressure rising and heart racing, I took a more direct approach. "We can't give our subordinates impossible tasks then punish them when they don't accomplish them." I followed this with an example that occurred earlier that morning in which my boss directed the department leaders to procure additional combat equipment for all of our vehicles. The directive stemmed from something he read somewhere, and it stated that every vehicle we owned should have this additional equipment. The problem was that it just was not realistic—only special forces units had this equipment, and we were not special forces.

As I was explaining the example, I asked if there was an underlying lesson he was trying to teach. "I want the additional equipment." Short and to the point. His response told me everything I needed to know. He was focused on himself and not on the greater good of the unit. But this conversation was still not over. I've had plenty of these courageous conversations in my career, but this one was just plain difficult. My anxiety at having this conversation was now combined with irritation and confusion. Respectfully, I responded, "Sir, at what cost? If you continue to treat our leaders this way, then you will lose them."

As it came out of my mouth, I wanted to take it back. Internally, I was cringing and bracing myself. I took a calculated risk by directly calling him out in the hopes that it would make him go to the balcony and see the consequences of his behavior. "I'm Commanding Officer, and everyone subordinate to me will do what I say, regardless of their morale or how they feel, and if they don't, they will be punished accordingly." And just like that, the conversation was over. I walked out.

The Marine Corps defines courage as: "a mental quality that recognizes fear of danger or criticism, but enables a Marine to proceed in the face of danger with calmness and firmness." While the Marine Corps may focus on the physical aspect of courage a bit more, and rightfully so, in the business world, we focus on moral courage, the ability to stand up and do what's right. Courage in business is a bit about calculated risk-taking—what are you willing to put a stake in the ground for? For Mike, having the difficult conversation with his boss was important. While it didn't end with the outcome he was hoping for, it did increase his confidence in having these conversations with his boss in the future. Courage in leadership can be demonstrated in both big ways, such as the CEO of Southwest Airlines vowing not to lay off employees three days after September 11, 2001, and to start a profit-sharing plan, or small ways, such as standing up for a coworker who is often marginalized in meetings when no one else will.

In his book, *Notes to the Future*, Nelson Mandela stated, "I learned that courage was not the absence of fear, but the triumph over it. I felt fear more times than I can remember, but I hid it behind a mask of boldness." In his book, *God Had a Dream*, Archbishop Desmond Tutu wrote, "Courage is not the absence of fear, but the ability to act despite it." What do these two leaders know that can benefit us all? That you can be scared in business, but the mark of a true leader is overcoming that fear and doing the right thing. Being courageous shouldn't be confused with being impulsive. Courage in leadership is about being bold, deliberate, and prepared.

Why is Courage in Leadership Important?

Leadership isn't an invitation-only club for people to join. We all have the ability to be great leaders. When you decide you want to be a leader, you start a journey of getting outside of your comfort zone and being uncomfortable. You commit to making decisions. You agree to empower others. You follow your values. All of these things take courage, especially in today's society where many are fearful of losing their jobs if they disagree with a decision or go against the grain, so to speak. There is no rule book for leadership. When COVID-19 hit, leaders didn't know what to do or how to react. They needed to create a new path for the very first time. Some leaders stepped up to the challenge, while others didn't, like our aerospace CEO from Chapter 5. Leaders need to make tough decisions. Everyone won't necessarily agree with these decisions. Sometimes these decisions may negatively impact others, including you, but they are the right decisions to make. Courage is being able to make these decisions.

Courage in business is about withstanding difficulty, the ability to persevere. As we've mentioned before, leadership is a marathon.

Leaders will have many battles along the way, and part of being a leader is the ability to know which battles are worth pursuing and which are not. Courage plays a few roles in leadership.

Courage builds trust. One of the fastest ways to increase influence and build trust is by being authentic. That means having the courage to show others not only your strengths, but your weaknesses as well. You need to be brave and honest in all interactions, which isn't always easy.

Courage builds accountability. A big reason it's often difficult for leaders to hold others accountable is because it can be uncomfortable to confront them, and the leader fears the response. By engaging in an open, honest, and respectful dialogue, courage allows leaders to call each other out and to hold others, and themselves, accountable.

Courage builds conflict capabilities. Most of us don't enter into a conversation thinking about how we can incite a conflict. In fact, we often shy away from conflict because we're scared of what may happen. By not addressing a situation or problem, we are complicit in our duties as leaders and are basically saying we're okay with the bad behaviors. Courage allows us to embrace the fear and challenge others with the hopes of coming to a resolution. These challenges are positive and spark necessary conversations.

Courage builds moral conviction. It's easy to turn a blind eye when we see wrongdoing, even when it conflicts with our values. We can easily fall into the bystander effect, where we think someone else will deal with it, so we don't have to. Courage gives leaders the strength to speak up when there is a values misalignment, bad behavior, or a toxic environment.

The ultimate outcome of courage is a sense of trust, engagement, and moral conviction that is created within a team. It also builds our capacity to take risks because often speaking out is a form of risk-taking, especially if it goes against popular belief. So what are some characteristics of a courageous leader?

Characteristics of a Courageous Leader

It's clear that courage in leadership is a critical trait. It's not about stepping in front of a bullet, like in the military, although there could be proverbial bullets that we may need to dodge in order to do our jobs effectively. Courage is about the power of our convictions being strong enough to move us to action. It's about having the moral courage to stand up for something that is unpopular or something that may harm us. Some characteristics of a courageous leader include:

Facing reality. Think about a leader you've had who saw the world through rose-colored glasses. Everything was always positive or "meant to be" or would "work out," even when tough decisions needed to be made. Did you feel like this leader was unable to stand up for you and your team because of these rose-colored glasses? By removing these glasses, leaders can face reality. It's important to see *what is* in order to determine what you need to do and what decisions need to be made. This isn't to say leaders shouldn't focus on the positive. Rather, be realistic and focus on the positive outcome of what you can achieve and what may need to be said or done in the process.

Saying what needs to be said. Leadership involves having awkward conversations about someone's performance, behavior, attitude, etc. These conversations are never easy and no one really looks forward to them. However, leaders need to embrace them. In our experience, situations only escalate and become worse when they aren't dealt with. Leaders who avoid the elephant in the room aren't doing themselves or their teams any favors. These often difficult conversations are called "crucial" or "courageous" conversations for a reason. They take courage to have. In our consulting work, courageous conversations are a very popular and often requested training topic. These tough conversations need to occur and allow leaders to get to the heart of the issue and move to resolution. Without having the conversations and without saying what needs to be said, the problem persists and gets worse. Leaders need to move to resolution as quickly as possible.

What Not to Wear

I was excited and was feeling really good about myself as I put on my uniform and made the short walk to the barber shop. It was my first day as a battalion executive officer, or second-in-command. I assisted the battalion commander in leading over 1,000 combat-ready Marines. I felt important and good about myself. As I walked, I passed several Marines. They all said good morning and continued walking past. But, they all gave me the same strange look. I couldn't quite figure out what was going on but, sensing something was off, I quickly looked down at my uniform, thinking something might be wrong. Everything looked correct. When I made it to the barber shop, it was still closed, so I sat and waited. A young Marine, fresh out of boot camp, meekly approached me. After exchanging the obligatory "good mornings," the young Marine fumbled a bit and apologetically informed me that my boots were not bloused. Basically, the proper way to wear this particular uniform was to use an elastic device to tuck or fold the end of the trousers back allowing more of the boot to be seen and giving the impression of a blouse, hence the term "blousing." Since World War One, Marines had bloused their boots to keep bugs and critters from crawling up the trouser legs. At this point, I had bloused my trousers thousands of times in my career. A Marine of any rank, forgetting to do this is considered "out of uniform not to mention it just looks silly because blousing is part of the uniform.

Now it finally made sense. The funny looks from the Marines who had passed me before. Those Marines, and others, significantly more senior than the young Marine standing in front of me, had let me walk around like that without stopping to confront and correct me. Instead, I just kept getting one funny look after another.

This young junior-level Marine had the moral courage to come up to me and respectfully point out the issue. I was so thankful and extended my appreciation to him with a great deal of humility. I asked for the young Marine's name and unit so I could contact his superiors and inform them of what a positive example he was.

I often say that, at times, demonstrating moral courage may be just as tough, if not tougher, than demonstrating physical courage. This young Marine was a prime example of that.

—*Story as told by Colonel Nick Nuzzo,*
United States Marine Corps

Encouraging healthy debate. Many leaders can feel pressured to know all of the answers. When you realize that you don't need to have all of the answers, you can encourage healthy debate and dissent on your team or within project groups. These conversations always remain respectful, with the end goal of coming to the best solution. When leaders welcome questions and are open to differing opinions, they are also saying they trust in the collective knowledge and the diversity of experience in their team. One way to encourage this type of healthy debate, as a leader, is by avoiding giving your opinion first. This is especially true when you manage people. Others can feel fearful about speaking up and disagreeing if they have a differing opinion. If you are trying to create a courageous culture, ask others for their opinions and thoughts first. Then when someone provides an idea, be encouraging and welcome the debate: "That's an interesting idea. What do others think? Could this work? Why or why not?" By doing this, you are opening the door to other opinions.

Standing on the skinny branch. A number of years ago, Hema worked for an organization where a leader in the Learning and Development department would often say, "Who is willing to walk on the skinny branch?" In many leadership-development classes, people do not like to speak first. This was basically her way of asking "Who is courageous enough to put themselves out there and share a story first?" Being a courageous leader requires walking on the skinny branch and being able to stand alone. The next time you are in a group meeting, go out on the skinny branch and offer your opinion or idea. Be the first person to start the discussion. This can also work in conversations with your manager. If you are in a one-on-one meeting and have something to say, say it. Ask for more responsibility. Ask for a raise. And then stand by your ask by providing examples as to why you would like more responsibility or more money. Be prepared to explain where you are coming from. Remember, you won't know unless you ask.

Being vulnerable. Courageous leaders know, own, and express their emotions in a healthy way. As Brené Brown states, "There is no courage without vulnerability." Many people believe that business is no place for emotions. The truth is, it's hard to remove our emotions from our work. For leaders, it's often seen as a sign of weakness to be vulnerable. It takes courage to be vulnerable, to admit you may not know something and to admit you're wrong. Doing any of these things doesn't make you any less of a leader. In fact, others view this as leadership. Leaders who are vulnerable can create an environment that encourages vulnerability in others and the ability to be authentic. Ultimately, being authentic and our true selves is what we're all after.

Willing to make mistakes. In Chapter 5, we talked about the ability to make decisions and pointed out that the decisions leaders make don't always have to be right. Courage in leadership is about the willingness to try, even if that decision is ultimately a mistake. Leaders need to overcome fear around making the wrong decision. Rather than not making any decision at all, leaders need to find the courage to move forward, make a decision, and then course correct if something happens. Courageous leaders do not have regret as they are willing to try.

Leading change. As we've said before, courage isn't the absence of fear. Rather, it's the ability to keep moving forward and driving change, especially in an organization that fears change. Maintaining the status quo is easy. But doing what you've always done doesn't produce different and potentially better results. Courageous leaders envision a better way, a better process, a better solution, and they find a way to make the future better. Change is messy, but courageous leaders bring people along on the journey and they course-correct as necessary.

Underlying all characteristics of courage is the ability to take risks. Courageous leaders would rather take the risks and fail than not take the risks at all. These are calculated risks because a good leader weighs the pros and cons before leaping. Courage is not closing your eyes and blindly jumping off the cliff, hoping you survive. Hope is not a strategy and courage is not a trait to be used as an excuse for leaders to take unrealistic risks.

Putting It into Practice

If you are content with the status quo and if where you are today professionally and personally is *good enough*, then you most likely haven't been practicing courageous leadership. To be honest, if the status quo is all you're looking for, we're surprised you've read this far. But, if you're someone who wants to elevate your leadership and your career and level of engagement in the process, then below are a few things you can start doing today.

Learn to say "I don't know." Leaders don't know everything, and that's perfectly okay. When asked a question, be honest if you don't know the answer and say so. Fumbling through an answer or making something up could be detrimental to your reputation and brand. It takes courage to admit when you don't know something. However, make a commitment to find out and get back to the person.

Set the bar high. We should all have personal and professional goals that we are working toward. Set a goal or a standard that makes you a little (or a lot) scared. Goals and expectations shouldn't be safe. If they are, then how will you set yourself apart from the crowd and how will you grow? Commit to setting one personal goal that seems nearly unattainable. Push yourself at work too. When you reach your goal, not only will you be surprised, but chances are you will want to keep pushing the bar higher and higher.

Do one thing you've been avoiding. We're not talking about things like doing your taxes, although you probably should take care of that if you've been putting them off. We're talking about things like conversations or big projects. Is there someone in your life, maybe at work or even in a personal relationship, who you've been avoiding because you want to address a concern or talk about an issue? If so, set a date and commit to having the discussion by then. Perhaps there's a project you need to get started on but have been procrastinating because you don't know where or how to start. You need to ask for assistance or clarification. Now is the time to do that! These acts take courage as they get you outside of your comfort zone.

The more you exercise courage in your daily life, the more you inspire others and the stronger you become as a leader. Courage takes many forms, and in business, it's more about stepping outside of your comfort zone. It's awkward at first, but much like everything else, take it slow. You have to learn to walk before you can run.

CHAPTER 12

KNOWLEDGE

Understanding of a science or an art. The range of one's information, including professional knowledge and understanding of your Marines.

I was blind. My face felt like I had dunked it in lava. I could hardly breathe, and I could hear the screams of the other Marines. I had just been sprayed directly in the eyes with oleoresin capsicum (OC) spray, or pepper spray. The first few moments were manageable and then it hit me. I tried to open my eyes so I could see how many fingers the instructor was holding up, and it felt like broken glass was under my eyelids. I now know why everyone dreaded this particular day in Marine Security Guard training.

Identifying the correct number of fingers the instructor was holding up was just the beginning. I ran to the first station to perform various upper-body strikes. Adrenaline was coursing through my body as I threw punch after punch. I was motivated to get through the six stations as fast as possible so I could rinse my face. I held nothing back and did my best to focus on technique. I knew if I didn't, the instructors would make me start over again, which meant I would get sprayed again. No thank you. With the instructor satisfied that I had properly demonstrated the required punches, I sprinted to the next station. The instructor called out the type of kick to be demonstrated. Fortunately, I quickly visualized the movement and started pounding the striking bag with each kick. The Marine holding the bag lost his balance. I was like a raging bull on a mission. A mission to get this spray off of my face!

I finally made it to the last, and most challenging, station. The other stations were basic strikes, kicks, and movements that we had done thousands of times before. This final station was different. The instructor would call out a takedown procedure that we needed to execute on another Marine, not a striking bag. It was a true test of fighting mastery—trying to keep your mind focused while the spray continued its way into your eyes. "Arm-bar takedown" was the movement the instructor wanted to see me perform. With my face, and now my neck, still feeling like they were on fire, I instinctively grabbed the Marine I was demonstrating the movement on by the wrist. All I heard next was, "Go to the water hose." I was finally done.

Later that day, with my eyes still burning, but not quite as badly, I thought about the training and why it was important that we went through it. Before we used the spray on another person, we had to know what the effects were. We had to feel them. Figure out how to maneuver while feeling the burn. Plus, in the event someone was to spray us, we knew how to function and continue performing our duties.

Luckily, most of us will never be sprayed in the eyes with OC spray. But this portion of the training was all about increasing knowledge. The Marine Corps defines knowledge as, "Understanding of a science or an art. The range of one's information, including professional knowledge and understanding of your Marines." OC spray sounds like neither an art or science, but it definitely did increase professional knowledge.

The business world defines knowledge in much the same way: understanding of a subject matter in order to effectively do your job. Knowledge stems from multiple sources, including personal and professional development, and also includes your experience. All of these sources combine to help you achieve your goals.

Knowledge is deeper than just *knowing* something. Leaders must use the knowledge and apply it appropriately based on the current operating environment. It's about the difference between theory and practice. We all know people who are very intelligent. They can recite facts and figures about science, history, business, and a host of other topics. But unless circumstances are ideal, they are unsure how to apply their knowledge to the actual situation. In leadership, this is detrimental to the team and the organization, not to mention to your own brand and reputation as a leader. The good news is, you are in control of keeping your knowledge current, figuring out how to make it relevant, and, better still, your knowledge stays with you regardless of where you work.

Three Types of Knowledge

There are three types of knowledge. Each is important in its own way, and you tap into each type of knowledge depending on the situation.

Expert knowledge. Are you the only one in your organization who can perform a certain task because you're the only one who knows how? Or do you have a high level of knowledge about a particular software platform, process, or procedure? Are you considered a subject-matter expert? If you answered yes, then you have expert knowledge in those specific areas. People come to you, not because you're dependable or reliable (although both could be true), but because you know how to do something others do not. Expert knowledge is a type of power. It gives you an edge over others, and you become a valuable resource. It's important to remember that expert knowledge should be relevant to your team and your organization. Think about a particular knowledge set that you possess within your organization. What value does that bring? Do others know that you are a knowledge expert in that area? If not, who should know, and how will you make it known? Part of establishing yourself as a leader is sharing your capabilities and knowledge with others.

Informational knowledge. Do you know what's happening on your team and within your organization? Are you aware of the company's direction, vision, and future plans? If the answer is yes, then you have valuable informational knowledge about your organization that many who aren't "in the know" may find useful. You can use informational knowledge to become the "go-to" source for others who want to know what is happening. However, as a leader, you need to share the information with discretion. Your manager and leadership team trust you enough to share information. Some of this information may be confidential or sensitive. Be sure not to lose the trust of others—share only what is useful. One place we find informational knowledge is around layoffs or reductions in force. Generally, Human Resources and managers in the organization are the first to know when there will be a layoff. They are called upon to help assess their employees and determine who may need to be laid off and who will stay. They are privy to this information weeks ahead of the actual reduction taking place. Managers often have one or two trusted employees on their teams whose opinions they value. This "inner circle" may know about the layoffs while others do not. If you are a leader who knows what is occurring, it can be difficult not to share, especially if a friend is being impacted. However, the ability to use discretion with what information you share is critical to continuing to be viewed as a leader.

Institutional knowledge. Think about an employee who has been at your organization the longest. Theoretically, they should have a deep understanding of the company, the policies, procedures, products, services, etc. They should also know the best communication routes, chains of command, and overall history of the organization. When was the last time you talked to this person? Many leaders want to start a new position or a new job like a bull in a china shop, disregarding everything that has been done before because they want to leave their own mark. The problem is, they disregard the institutional knowledge held by members of the team and the understanding these employees have of what's been tried in the past, why it was successful, and why it may have failed. Institutional knowledge is a deep expertise in your specific organization. A strong leader must be an expert in the company and in the business. While you can't take this knowledge with you, unless you're going to a competitor, it is extremely useful in your time at an organization.

Leaders must possess all three types of knowledge to truly be successful. Each serves a different purpose and each is used differently within the organization to make decisions. In fact, some organizations, like GE, require employees to be in their positions for a specified number of years before they are even eligible for promotion. This allows people to become true experts in their areas, and they are better equipped to handle the responsibilities and challenges that come with the next role or level.

But Why is Having All of This Knowledge so Important?

Have you ever worked for someone who had absolutely no idea what you did as part of your job? They had never been in your role, walked in your shoes, or encountered the situations you face. How did you feel about this leader? In our experience, you end up resenting the leader, not understanding how they even made it to their position or level without the technical expertise. You can be a leader in terms of being motivational, visionary, decisive, and courageous, but if you don't have the technical knowledge to lead your team, none of those other attributes matter. As a leader, how will you critically assess a problem or strategically think about how to solve it if you lack the specific technical expertise to effectively assist? A number of years ago, Hema worked for a leader who didn't understand talent management. The previous leader understood the nuances and knew enough to be dangerous. While she may not have been an expert, she had enough knowledge to remove obstacles if they arose. The new leader was unable to do this, and Hema had to navigate the obstacles without guidance.

Many leaders believe that as long as they surround themselves with strong technical experts, they do not need to possess the domain knowledge. This couldn't be further from the truth. First, if you, as a leader, lack the technical knowledge, how do you know when you've surrounded yourself with experts? Second, if the experts are providing information, how can you as the leader effectively evaluate it?

When you process information, you gain knowledge. You become aware of the realities of the situation or circumstances. This connection to reality, combined with the ability to engage the information when needed is why knowledge is important to leadership. A leader needs to be able to tap into this to make decisions, to speak intelligently about a topic, and to navigate roadblocks and obstacles. In addition, knowledge allows you to be decisive, use judgment, and be reliable in order to accomplish the task or mission at hand. Leaders know that gaining knowledge isn't a one-time task.

Leaders are Lifelong Learners

As we've mentioned before, leaders need to act. When they receive new information, they must react and make decisions. With information constantly changing and new and innovative software, trends, etc., there is no shortage of new things to learn or be aware of. In order to remain effective, leaders need to keep up, and the only way to do so is to be a lifelong learner—always learning something new, updating the knowledge library that exists in their heads.

The world we live in requires us to constantly be able to connect the dots. Leaders especially need to be able to make connections that others can't see. Part of being able to do this is to anticipate what is going to happen next, what is coming in the future. Unlike a crystal ball, it's less about psychic abilities and more about continuously reading and gaining valuable insights and knowledge in order to predict what's coming. For example, think about artificial intelligence (AI). While AI has been in existence for a while, leaders at Apple and Amazon saw a way to bring AI into homes through

Siri and Alexa. Talent Acquisition and Human Resources leaders are bringing AI more into their hiring and recruiting to streamline their efforts because they know an investment in this type of technology can make them more efficient and effective in the long term. Some people are in the "wait and see" bucket. They may be aware of what is out there. Other leaders are in the "first mover" bucket. They are up-to-date on the latest trends and have connected the dots as to how a new technology or process could benefit their organization. They have done the analysis to predict the future and can show the value of being innovative or changing a process or procedure. Others in the organization trust in their judgment because their analysis and decisions are based in knowledge versus pure opinion.

Here are a few questions to consider on your path to becoming a lifelong learner:

How much time this week have you invested in learning something or becoming a better leader? This can be reading a book (like this one!), listening to relevant podcasts, or even researching online.

Who are the people you need to learn from? There are always people ahead of us. Rather than getting jealous of their success or where they may be in life, think about how you can learn from them. Clearly, what they've been doing has been successful.

In your current job, what specific areas require subject-matter expertise or a deep understanding? Think about the last decision you made that required this expert knowledge. Think about how you made the decision you did.

What additional knowledge do you still need to gain in order to move up in your career? This can be expert, informational, or institutional knowledge

The Shaky Gun

"Shooters, load your weapons!"

This was the command that I gave to my four Marines and the two men from the Nepalese Army. Then I heard one of my Marines yell my name while waving his arms in the air. I walked over and asked him if everything was alright. He pointed to the Nepalese man next to him, whose pistol had fallen apart in his hands. The man looked at me confused and began speaking in Nepalese, which I wasn't exactly fluent in. Luckily, we had a translator nearby, and I asked him to tell the Nepalese man to keep calm and that we would figure it out.

Then the Nepalese man pointed the gun to his face and looked down the wrong end of the barrel; he didn't see or understand that the bullet was still in the barrel and he could end up shooting himself in the face or hurting someone else. Instinctively, I grabbed the barrel from the man's hand and explained that there was a live bullet in the chamber.

Thinking I was going to help him put his gun back together, he handed me the rest of his completely disassembled pistol. I had never seen, or even heard of, this brand of gun, but now everyone was looking to me to fix it. I needed to rely on my knowledge and understanding of basic pistol nomenclature to figure this out. I asked one of my Marines to hold some of the extra pieces so I could reassemble one section of the pistol at a time. After a couple of minutes, I managed to put the pistol back together, and then I noticed why it had fallen apart in the first place. The lever that was supposed to keep the two main components together was worn to the point it would not lock into place. At this point, I told the translator that the weapon could not be fired and to do so would be dangerous. I showed the translator and the Nepalese man the worn lever. The pistol then broke again. I quickly reassembled it one more time, handed it back to the Nepalese man and told him he could not fire it. That it was a danger to himself and those around him. I could see the look of disappointment in the man's eyes after the translator had finished explaining the situation. I asked him if he would like to shoot my pistol, and I could see a large grin on his face. After walking him through how to properly load and shoot it, we resumed shooting, incident free.

Being a lifelong learner isn't just about increasing technical knowledge. It's also about keeping up with changes in leadership, the skills needed to be an effective leader, and developing an understanding of how different employees like to be communicated with or what drives them.

In addition to technical knowledge, leaders need to know their people. Think back to the Marine Corps definition of knowledge, "...understanding of your Marines." Every employee is different and therefore should be treated as an individual. How you communicate with one person may not necessarily be how you communicate with everyone. Think about personal relationships. Do you communicate the same way with each person? Are your conversations generic, or do you know what is going on in your friend's lives so the conversations are tailored and personal? Chances are, it's the latter.

Awareness of what is happening in the lives of those around us is a form of knowledge. It's aligned with *informational knowledge*. This knowledge helps further relationships and increases trust between you and your friend. The same is true in leadership. When you get to know your colleagues at every level of the organization, you can have deeper relationships with them and build trust. Remember, this trust is important to being viewed as a leader, someone who others can count on.

When you manage people, getting to know your direct reports is essential. Not only does this build trust with each team member, but it also improves performance. People want to be recognized and they want to know their manager sees them. This can be as simple as asking how someone's weekend was. You get a feel for the types of activities they like, whether they have pets, if they prefer to stay home and relax. Questions like these are conversation starters. When asking these questions, show interest. Remember to be in level two or level three listening. If you don't remember the difference, take a look back at Chapter 1. Trust us, it's important! In addition, you increase engagement and loyalty to the team and organization.

Here are a few questions to consider asking your employees to get to know them better. Some of these questions are best in a one-on-one meeting so you can build a better relationship with one another.

What gets you excited to come to work in the morning? This question will provide insight into someone's motivation and what they value.

What books have you read recently that you would recommend? You can also recommend a book that you've enjoyed.

What shows or movies have you watched on Netflix? While this may sound trivial, it's all about getting to know someone, and you want others to be comfortable with you.

What is one accomplishment you are proudest of? Stay positive with your questions. The goal is to get people to think and open up while remaining engaged and positive.

Remember, taking the time to get to know your employees is a way of showing that you value them. This value leads to an increase in trust. When employees trust their leader, they are willing to work extra hard and do their best.

Gaining knowledge, whether technical or otherwise, is positive and serves us well in our roles personally and professionally. However, there is such a thing as too much knowledge.

Analysis Paralysis

The term is synonymous with knowing too much and not being able to effectively make a decision. Think back to decisiveness for a second. Have you ever worked with someone who, instead of making a decision, kept asking for more information? They kept increasing their knowledge while not getting any closer to a decision. It's like running on a treadmill; you can run for miles and get nowhere. Leaders cannot afford to be stuck in analysis paralysis. It's a productivity killer. To avoid this cycle of researching and overanalyzing, set a deadline for when you need to make a decision and stop researching! Then, when you are researching, determine what data is actually needed. It's easy to keep gathering data and then have no use for it. Instead, focus on data and information that is aligned with the goal you are trying to accomplish. This will help move you from analysis paralysis to smart analysis.

Don't Be a Hoarder

We can't move on without a quick word about being a knowledge hoarder. Think about a time when you may have been a knowledge hoarder. What was the circumstance? Why did you feel like you couldn't share the information? We all know at least one knowledge hoarder. They have the intelligence. They have the expertise. They have the know-how. They have the information. However, they are unwilling to share their knowledge for a variety of reasons. Sometimes, knowledge hoarders are scared that if they share what they know, then they become less valuable and less needed. In effect, they can be replaced. The truth is, we are all replaceable within our organizations. But how can you expect your organization to grow if you aren't willing to share what you know?

Knowledge hoarders have a lack of trust in those around them. They find it hard to see the big picture and are focused on their narrow view. Leaders cannot afford to be knowledge hoarders, whether intentionally or unintentionally. If you find yourself feeling reluctant to share knowledge when asked (and we're not talking about sensitive and confidential information), ask yourself why. Gain self-awareness as to the circumstances causing this behavior. Then determine how to pivot and become a knowledge sharer, which is what all leaders need to be.

Putting It into Practice

It's commonly known that Warren Buffet spends five to six hours a day reading. Bill Gates reads up to fifty books per year. President

Obama carves out at least one to two hours daily to read. These leaders know that increasing their knowledge is key to making the best decisions and to keep moving forward. Below are a few things you can start doing today to help you increase your knowledge.

Be patient. We mentioned earlier that companies like GE are requiring employees to stay in positions for a specified number of years before they are eligible for promotion. This is because they see the value in gaining the knowledge to do the job extremely well. This takes patience and an ability to build time in the job. When you jump one position to the next or are quickly promoted, you have to start over every time. Instead, build a strong foundation in your current role, gain the experience, increase your knowledge, use it to make impactful decisions, and get recognized. Others will see your actions and behaviors, and they will respect you more as you move up the corporate ladder.

Build learning agility. Dive deep into your industry and your business. Don't just skim the surface. Take the time to meet people in other departments within your organization. Attend conferences. Read more about the issues and opportunities your industry faces and spend time thinking about how you can contribute to either solving those issues or achieving those opportunities. By increasing your knowledge of your industry and your organization, you are better equipped to have intelligent conversations and healthy debates with others. You are establishing yourself as knowledgeable in your domain and open to sharing that information. This behavior gets noticed, and when there are stretch opportunities or new projects, you could be tapped on the shoulder.

Learn something new. Many organizations have an internal Learning Management System (LMS) or other learning and development system. Ask your Human Resources department what your organization offers. Courses can range from position-specific content to general leadership. You can also talk with your manager. Often, each department has a professional development budget. This may also be an opportunity to learn something adjacent to your job—a skill you may not need immediately, but will be beneficial to your career in the future and to the organization. You can also take up a new hobby. Learning how to play the violin or learning how to cook are all ways to increase your knowledge and develop a lifelong learner mindset. It's up to you to take the initiative and move to action.

Many of us wouldn't think of knowledge as a leadership trait. We would consider it something we have or don't have. The truth is, your level of knowledge and how you use it are key to who you are as a leader.

CHAPTER 13

LOYALTY

*The quality of faithfulness to country, Corps, unit,
seniors, subordinates, and peers.*

I was talking to a group of my Marines when I heard "Cease Fire!" over the radio. Those are words that an artillery unit never wants to hear. They usually mean that a unit fired a round in the wrong location, otherwise known as a "firing incident." Such was the case on this occasion as well, but the real problem was that it was my unit that had the firing incident. Before shooting, the Marines were provided with the coordinates of where they need to aim and shoot. In this case, the wrong coordinates had been relayed to the Marines, and the round landed nearly two and a half miles from the intended target. Luckily, no one was hurt or injured from the incident.

Firing incidents are always difficult, even when there are no injuries. My boss had to explain how this happened to his boss, the colonel. There was already friction between the two. This was not going to make it any better.

I could hear the colonel giving an earful to my boss over the phone. I felt bad for him, as he was doing everything he could to lead and teach the Marines proper firing procedures. I should know. I had been there through all of it. The difficult part was that I also understood the colonel's position as well—my boss was responsible for everything that happened, good or bad. The buck stopped with him.

Later that day, the colonel pulled me aside, catching me off guard. He wanted to know my thoughts on my boss. Was he doing his job as a leader? Did he have control of the unit? I had a sneaking suspicion that the colonel wanted me to give him details—something, anything that he could then use to remove my boss from command, essentially firing him. This put me in a very awkward position. On one side, the success of my unit depended on the trust and loyalty between my boss and I. We had to be loyal to one another and have each other's backs in order to succeed. On the other side, if the colonel didn't like what I had to say, he could end my career as well.

There was really only one thing I could do: tell the truth. I told the colonel that my boss had the respect of each Marine in the unit and they would follow him anywhere. That he was the hardest working Marine in the unit and that he would take responsibility for this incident and learn from it. While he wasn't the one who caused the miscalculation in coordinates, he was ultimately accountable, and he would teach everyone else about the incident in order to not repeat it. Not only was my boss devoted to the Marines, he was devoted to the Marine Corps and to doing the right thing. This was the type of leader I was committed to. Luckily, my response satisfied the colonel, and I could see the tension in his face lighten.

The Marine Corps defines loyalty as, "The quality of faithfulness to country, Corps, unit, seniors, subordinates, and peers." Clearly, I have been fortunate to be surrounded by some of the best leaders, who inspire loyalty in others. The business world defines loyalty in much the same way as the Marine Corps. In business, we look at loyalty through various lenses. First, as a leader, do you have a loyal following? Second, as an employee, how loyal are you to your leader? Lastly, whether leader or employee, how loyal are you to your organization? All of these lenses are important when talking about leadership. After all, if no one else thinks you're a leader and no one is following you, then are you really a leader?

Early in our careers, we may not consider loyalty an important leadership trait. We may be more focused on our pay, benefits, or other perks the organization offers. But finding excellent talent and having them stay with your organization is becoming increasingly difficult. As leaders focus on growing in their careers and employees focus on finding the right organizational culture, we see a lot of turnover within organizations. In our "What have you done for me lately?" society, loyalty is becoming scarcer. Great leaders know that loyalty is the cornerstone of their leadership; they need to earn the loyalty of others, and they need to give loyalty to others.

Why Loyalty is Important

Have you ever had a colleague who agreed with you and had your back in private but, when asked in a public setting, was quick to throw you under the bus? How did you feel about them afterwards? Did you still trust them? We've had this happen in our careers, and it doesn't feel good. In addition to tarnishing a friendship or working relationship, it makes you question their loyalty, and you no longer trust them. Now, imagine if that colleague was your manager!

Would you really remain high performing and committed at work, or would you be looking for a new job?

Loyalty in leadership is one way to avoid costly turnover. But, it's deeper than that. It's about creating an emotional connection with those around you. So, why does loyalty matter in leadership?

It builds your brand. If you want to become a memorable leader, you need to have a following. This following should be average and above-average employees. These employees give you instant credibility. There's a reason they are following you. Plus, these employees wouldn't be following you if you weren't a strong leader and a good human being. You're indirectly communicating to others that you know what you're doing.

Mistakes can be forgiven. Even the best leaders make mistakes. As we've mentioned before, you can make a decision, but it may not always be the right one. Your employees and peers are more apt to forgive you if they know you will do the same for them. In fact, one sure-fire way to build loyalty is to always have the back of each team member, especially when things don't go right.

The truth is more important than a lie. Loyal employees are more open and honest and will tell you the truth. This isn't just in an employee-to-manager relationship, but in peer-to-peer relationships as well. We all need to hear the truth. It makes us better people and better leaders. It also helps in our decision-making ability. Loyal employees tap into the trust that exists in the relationship and use it to be honest. While this truth may hurt initially, the end result is what matters.

Loyalty is part of our daily habits. As a consumer, why do you shop a certain brand? Why do you keep going back to the same restaurant? You may like the quality of clothing, the quality of food, the ambience. Whatever the reason, you keep going back. That's loyalty. Loyalty in leadership is similar. People follow you for a reason. They keep coming back for more.

Why Do People Follow You?

So, why *do* people follow you? There are two paths to choose: trust-based loyalty or fear-based loyalty. Which one sounds better? Trust-based loyalty is what you want. This is the loyalty we mentioned above, the one based on mutual respect and trust. This is the obvious reason people should want to follow you and the reason you should want people to follow you. Sadly, it's not the reason many people have "followers."

Fear-based loyalty is the exact opposite of trust-based loyalty. Think schoolyard bully. Fear-based loyalty is imposing trust versus earning it. It's using your title to get what you want. It's making threats so people do what you say because they are scared. That's not leadership, but it is a common occurrence.

Earlier in her career, Hema worked for a CEO just like this. He used his title and the fact that he owned the company to bully employees and put them down. Employees were scared to lose their pay, bonus opportunities, and even their jobs. He not only bullied employees but clients and prospective clients as well, trying to make them bend to his will and using threats to get his way. Eventually, it caught up with him; his employees left, and the business shut down.

If you've created fear-based loyalty, then you've created a fear-based culture. Can you think of a colleague who you have worked with, or even heard about, in your organization who threatens people or uses their position or seniority to get their way? This is the person who you don't want to talk to or interact with, but need to in order to effectively do your job. We often wonder how this person still has their job and what compromising information they have on the boss or organization that allows their behavior to be tolerated. Throughout our careers, we have known a few people like this. We're sure you do too. In these fear-based cultures, employees aren't giving their best, and the second a better opportunity comes along, they are gone.

So, how can you tell whether people follow you out of trust or fear? Answer these questions honestly.

Do you surround yourself with only people who think like you and share your views?

Do you avoid asking for feedback because it doesn't matter to you or you don't care what others have to say?

Is your team a revolving door of talent? Is someone always leaving the first chance they get?

Is your team stagnant and not growing?

If you answered yes to these questions, then chances are you are working in a fear-based environment with zero loyalty. The good news is, you can change this.

Habits That Inspire Loyalty

Think about customer loyalty programs. They are designed to keep people coming back for more. Leadership should be the same way. Here are some things you can do to inspire loyalty.

Be authentic. It's easy to tell whether someone is being fake or genuine, unless they are a really great actor. An authentic leader says what they mean, means what they say, and follows through. They do not change their behavior or decisions depending on the audience. We've all known people who are seemingly two different people depending on whether they are at work or at home, or talking to their peers versus their manager. We may even feel like we have a split personality sometimes. Not only can others see right through this behavior, it's exhausting to keep up. Being an authentic leader is about building your self-awareness, being comfortable not knowing something, and being open to hearing opinions that are different from your own.

Don't micromanage. Micromanaging is a quick way to erode trust and loyalty. Nobody likes someone constantly peering over their shoulder second-guessing their work. You don't have to manage employees to be a micromanager. Think back to when you were in school and doing a class project. Everyone had a piece to accomplish. Were you constantly checking in with others to see how they were doing on their portion and whether they needed help? Work projects are the same way. Trust that others will get their work done. Focus on your work and what you can control. As a people manager, checking in during one-on-ones or team meetings is normal, but don't cross the line into micromanaging.

Lead by example. Fear-based leaders come from the mindset of "do as I say, not as I do." Trust-based leaders, on the other hand, walk the walk and talk the talk. They are willing to do everything they are asking of others and do not feel they are above anyone else. When a leader is unwilling to roll up their sleeves and get their hands dirty, then others can feel as if their work is unimportant or trivial. If others see you jumping in to help and doing what it takes to make the company successful, they will do the same. Just be mindful that you don't step on toes in the process.

Be supportive. As a leader, have the backs of your team. Even if you disagree with a team member, hold the discussion one on one, outside of a group setting. While in a group setting, be supportive and trust that your team member is knowledgeable and using sound judgment. Outstanding leaders put people first, and they view their teams as people, not employees. Supportive leaders are not bullies, and they don't allow others to bully their team either. This is how great leaders forge strong bonds and relationships, adding to their following.

Take responsibility. In addition to not throwing others under the bus, strong leaders take ownership of what needs to be done. They ultimately hold themselves accountable. They do this by actively listening to others and following up. For example, if you tell your manager about an issue that you are facing or a decision you need help with, your manager can show accountability by following up with you on how it ultimately ended, what decision was made, and what can be done to help mitigate this setback in the future. Ultimately, your manager is accountable for the actions and behaviors of their team members. You can also take accountability by owning the outcome and being responsible for the decision-making process. You need to take responsibility for your role as a member of a team.

Focus on the long term. In the course of our everyday lives, whether personally or professionally, it can be easy to focus on the short-term outcomes or get frustrated by minor roadblocks. Leadership is about focusing on the long term and the bigger picture. Our first reaction can be to get angry at a coworker who was late to a meeting or who came in late to work. In the grand scheme of things, how much does it matter? It most certainly isn't worth calling them out publicly. Instead, pull them aside later and ask them if everything is okay. If it is, then keep moving forward on the larger goals that you're trying to accomplish.

Loyal to the Core

Things were finally becoming real. I had just finished coordinating my changeover ceremony, where my successor officially takes over from me, when my boss came into my office with a concerned look on his face. I knew this look—he was having an internal struggle about a decision. He told me that we had a very important command inspection and that he really wanted me to take the lead to coordinate and prepare the unit. It was a lot of responsibility and work. It would take up a lot of time, and I was focused on my upcoming retirement in just three short months. Truthfully, I was honored that he wanted me to lead it. It was also much more manageable than figuring out how to prepare a resume and interview. My boss's main concern was how much time I would dedicate to the inspection versus how much time I would spend working on my transition out of the Marine Corps. He wanted to ensure that I had a smooth transition. There was no way I was going to let him down, especially after he had gone out on a limb and chosen me to be a part of his command team. I told him not to worry and that I would put together a schedule for the inspection preparation. I knew I did not have to, but I wanted to help him as well as the other Marines in the unit. Anything I could do to help the unit in my final days in uniform, I was going to do. The

Marine Corps had been my home for twenty-three years, and I was committed to my Marines.

For the next three months, I balanced my transition out of the Marine Corps with preparing my unit for the inspection. I found that the time preparing the Marines for the inspection was a perfect way to end my career, doing what I love to do: teaching Marines. The unit's files and procedures were ready and only needed minor updates to be inspection ready. A bigger area of need I noticed was that some of the Marines had never been through an inspection. They didn't know that some of the inspectors view a lack of confidence as a lack of knowledge or an attempt to cover up an error. Since I would not be there to answer the inspector's questions, I wanted to prepare the Marines for how to present information and answer questions. I put each department and Marine through mock inspections over and over again, always challenging them and building their confidence. Although I wouldn't be there, my goal was to ensure the unit and the Marines would effectively pass the inspection. By the day of my retirement, the Marines were more than ready for the inspection.

A few months after retirement, my former boss called me and told me the inspection went well, and he was pleased by the results. He was grateful for my help. He also invited me to be his honored guest for a big unit event. I couldn't wait to go back and see everyone. Just because I was retired didn't mean that my devotion and loyalty to the Marine Corps went away.

Mike's retirement ceremony (March 16, 2018)

Be encouraging. Fear-based leaders don't want others to succeed. Their insecurities take over, and they would rather keep others down in order to make themselves look and feel better. Leaders who have a loyal following believe in the development of others. They encourage others to continuously learn something new or become better at their own crafts. They aren't afraid that someone else may have more knowledge than they do. In fact, it should be a sign of pride when someone you've managed is promoted and takes on more responsibility, especially if you are an engaged leader. They will be loyal to you and your leadership and will also stoke your brand and reputation as a leader. Additionally, it can be easy to feel jealous when coworkers or friends are promoted, especially if you weren't recently promoted. Someone else being promoted or having good fortune doesn't take away from you and what you offer. By encouraging others to go for a promotion or congratulating them when they get a promotion, you are showing that you aren't just focused on yourself and truly want what is best for others as well.

See people as people. When you take a genuine interest in the lives of your team, you are establishing a bond and building trust. However, if you view your team as pawns to be used to further your own interests, then building loyalty is the least of your issues. Take the time to show genuine interest and concern. Be empathetic if they are going through something. Don't focus solely on the work. All great leaders know that everyone has a life outside of work and those external factors impact work performance.

Over the past number of years, we've seen loyalty to employers decreasing. People are switching jobs frequently and chasing "the next big thing." However, this shouldn't affect your behavior. Remember, it's about focusing on the big picture and inspiring loyalty at all levels. This adds to your reputation as a leader, and you carry this brand with you throughout your career as well as your personal relationships.

How to Spot Loyalty

While it's important to be loyal as a leader, it's equally important to work for someone who is loyal as well. It's not always easy to spot the leaders with a loyal following. But, by asking a few questions, you can gain more insight that can help you.

What is the current tenure of team members under a particular leader? The goal is three years or more. It means people want to stick around, and the leader is doing something right.

Have others followed the leader from previous companies? Some of the best leaders will have a core group of people who want to follow them.

How many people have been promoted under this leader and then changed teams? It sounds funny to say because loyalty is about a following. But think about the trust and confidence the leader has in their team members to help them get promoted, knowing they will be losing a high performer? It's all about good karma!

How would team members describe the leader? It's one thing for a leader to tell you what their style is like. It's another to hear about it from your peers and those who report directly to the leader.

How visible is the leader? If they are sitting in their office all day and not interacting with the team, that could be a sign they don't have the best relationship with their team. In today's virtual environment, it can be harder to gauge this. One way to do so is to ask how the leader stays engaged with a remote team.

Ensuring your leader has a strong following is important to helping you build your own loyalty. A strong leader serves as a good role model. Observe their behaviors and think about how you may be able to incorporate some of them into your own leadership toolbox.

A Quick Word of Caution

We all have "go-to" people. Personally, these may be your two closest friends who you tell everything to and whose advice you seek when you have an issue. Professionally, these may be people who are reliable and dependable. They may be loyal to the organization and to you as a person and leader. Just as we mentioned with dependability, be careful that you aren't abusing someone's loyalty by asking them to take on additional responsibility. This can happen with colleagues who have been with an organization for a considerable length of time and who have weathered multiple storms. Managers may feel secure in asking this person to take on more because they haven't left so far, so chances are they aren't going anywhere. As a leader, ask yourself why you are asking someone to take on more responsibility and check in with them regarding their current workload. As someone who is often asked to take on more, don't always say yes. Saying no doesn't diminish your loyalty to your leader or organization. It makes you a stronger leader, assuming it's done tactfully, respectfully, and for good reason.

Also, as mentioned, a sign of a leader with a following is finding out how many people have followed them from a previous company. This is a double-edged sword. A number of years ago, Hema worked for an organization under a strong leader. Shortly after she started, there was turnover—the old leader was out and a new leader was coming on board. This new leader had a strong following…that eventually led to over 60% of the department being let go to make room for his people. While his following was loyal to him and he to them, it was more of an inner circle mentality—if you weren't in, then you were out. The manner in which changes were made and the judgment used was not aligned with a strong set of leadership core values, and things like institutional knowledge were dismissed. These situations do arise, and it's important to be aware of them. Keep the lines of communication open with the new leader and feel the situation out. If you don't feel aligned with the new leader, it may be time to find a new organization or new leader to be loyal to.

Putting It into Practice

The true test of loyalty in all relationships is what happens when things go wrong, as they inevitably will at some point. Do your followers have your back, or do they make a mad dash for the nearest exit? As we mentioned early on, loyalty has multiple lenses. One lens is how loyal team members are to a particular leader. A second lens is how loyal a leader is to their team. A third lens is how loyal a leader and team are to their organization. Whichever lens you look through, loyalty starts with you. Below are a few things you can do to help build a loyal following.

Take a look in the mirror. We have to turn the lens inward first. Check in with yourself to see how real or fake you are in any given circumstance. As you go through your day, keep a mental list of the times you felt more authentic and the times you felt like you were putting on a persona or character. Do this for a week to gather enough information to check for patterns. Are there certain times where you are more authentic? What are the circumstances in which you find yourself out of alignment with your authentic self? Also, go back and ask yourself the questions related to why people follow you. Take a self-assessment of whether you build trust-based loyalty or fear-based loyalty. We have to know where we're starting from before we can start to evolve our leadership.

Be a team player. Attend team meetings and social events. These are shared experiences that are designed to increase trust and build camaraderie. As a leader, your absence speaks volumes, and people do notice. While you may dread social gatherings, make it a habit to attend and set a goal for what you'd like to accomplish during the event. This may be getting to know a specific team member more or learning about hobbies that others enjoy. Additionally, be present for the crazy and hectic office moments as well. If there is a big project due or a deadline that needs to be met, ask what you can do to help. It may be nothing, but being available and checking in with the team is a sign of support and a feeling that everyone is in it together.

Include others. Building deep and long-lasting loyalty is about bringing others along the journey with you. Even if you *think* you have the answer or know the best route to take, ask others for their input and recommendations. This builds stronger bonds, and everyone feels like a part of a solution or project. Plus, it's a development opportunity as everyone can learn from one another. You gain buy-in and people feel valued.

Loyalty isn't a stand-alone leadership trait. It is built on dependability, tact, trust, honesty, and integrity. If, as a leader, one of these other characteristics is missing, loyalty is affected. Loyalty must be mutual. It takes time to build it and just a moment to destroy it.

CHAPTER 14

ENTHUSIASM

Motivation is contagious.

I was on 29 Palms, the largest training center for the Marine Corps, walking the long line of vehicles and talking to the Marines along the way, asking how they would spend their much-needed time off after the two-week training operation we'd just finished. Outside of one vehicle, I came across a young Marine who had joined the unit recently. With grease on his face and hands, he was still tirelessly working and he was happier than any of the other 149 Marines around him.

This young Marine must have seen me out of the corner of his eye because, before I could ask how he was doing, he dropped everything to render the appropriate military greeting—an enthusiastic, "Good afternoon, First Sergeant." His reaction caught me off guard—we had been in the field for over two weeks and were filthy and exhausted. His volume and energy, despite what we had just been through, was inspiring. At this point, he had my full attention. I asked him to tell me about himself and why he joined the Marine Corps. The stoic military presence gave way, and his true personality came out. It was as if a whole new fire had been set inside of him. I could already see why the other Marines in the unit had immediately accepted him as one of their own. Intrigued by his energy and story, I asked him what he was working on when I walked up. When all of the other Marines in the unit were either playing cards, reading, or otherwise relaxing, this Marine was still working.

He took my question as an opportunity to showcase what he knew and to teach me more about the weapon system. He was working on a howitzer, a complex weapon, and most of what the young Marine was telling me was going way over my head. But because of his enthusiasm, passion, and attitude, I was captivated, doing my very best to understand what he was telling me. At one point, he could see the confused look on my face, and he changed his teaching technique in an effort to help me understand better. The truth was, I was less focused on what he was saying and more focused on him. This Marine was special and had the elusive and hard to describe "it" factor.

The young Marine's energy and passion for the Marine Corps and his job were inspiring. It would have been easy for the young Marine to say as little as possible in the hopes that I would leave him alone. However, the young Marine wanted to share what he knew, and he wanted to make sure those he was teaching really understood. This experience was a complete role reversal, as normally I was the one teaching younger Marines. More than that, it was a humbling and proud moment for me—I was learning something new from a Marine much younger than me, whose character would take him far in his career. I was the leader who was supposed to be inspiring and teaching him, but on this day, he inspired and taught me.

This Marine encompassed the Marine Corps description of enthusiasm: "Motivation is contagious." On that day, and I'm sure on many others that followed, he motivated everyone around him. It seems funny to think of enthusiasm as a leadership trait. But in business, we describe enthusiasm in much the same way as the Marine Corps. When one person is motivated and excited, the entire attitude of a group can change. This is even truer when that person is the leader.

We all have difficult days, especially leaders, when work is stressful and deadlines are looming, and this is especially true of leaders. It's how leaders behave during these times that really helps define their leadership. As Hema matured as a leader, she would tap into this enthusiasm to keep the team moving forward on projects. While she was ultimately accountable for the success or failure of the final outcome, she knew she needed her team to be motivated to give their best, especially at the eleventh hour. This positivity and passion also helped Hema to keep moving forward and to ensure projects were successfully completed by the deadline.

Yes, enthusiasm sounds great in theory. But why is it critical in leadership?

Leadership is Predicated on Enthusiasm

Do you remember Eeyore from Winnie the Pooh? He was always so mopey. Nothing made him happy, and everything was always more negative than it was positive. We've all worked with people like this. Even after they say something positive, they quickly follow it up with "but…," and the negative shoe drops. While people like this make it difficult to have a high-performing team, imagine if your leader was like this! Not only would that team not be high performing, but there would most likely be a high level of turnover as well. Successful leadership is actually all about enthusiasm.

Enthusiasm inspires. Just like the Marine Corps definition states, *motivation is contagious.* Successful leaders inspire those around them through their passion. They love what they do and it shows. Their drive comes from within, and they want to share that with others. They want others to love what they do just as much. When you're around a leader who inspires, you want to be better and do better. Others see this and they follow suit. In addition, the vision or the "why" remain at the forefront, and this connects people to the work in an inspiring way as well.

Enthusiasm sets the tone. If you go into a situation negatively, chances are you will have negative results. On the other hand, if you go into it with a positive attitude, then the outcome is more likely to be positive. It's a bit of a self-fulfilling prophecy. Enthusiasm sets the tone for your experience. If you saw a TV commercial where someone was advertising a product less than enthusiastically with a careless tone and body language, would you be inspired to buy that product? We wouldn't. But, if that same product was advertised by someone who was super enthusiastic, there's a bigger likelihood that you would purchase it.

Enthusiasm achieves success. In the same vein that enthusiasm sets the tone, it also helps leaders achieve success. It's all about mindset. The more motivated you are to reach a positive outcome or goal, the more likely you will be to actually achieve it. While there still may be roadblocks along the way, enthusiasm allows you to move past those obstacles and focus on the finish line. You're excited about it and this excitement will keep you motivated and keep procrastination at bay.

Expressing enthusiasm is a choice. Not every situation we encounter is going to be a positive one. However, when you focus on why you are doing it, let your goal motivate you to keep moving forward. Much like with endurance, forward progress is critical and bringing others along on that journey is how a leader achieves success.

There are also some real benefits to being an enthusiastic leader. For starters, others want to follow you. We are more drawn to a leader who achieves goals and focuses on the positive than we are to someone who only sees problems or who is always critical. Another benefit is that your team delivers great results. They want to go the extra mile because they are motivated. As a result, you are also seen as a role model and more of a leader. This is how you build that following we talked about with loyalty. You gain a reputation as someone who can overcome obstacles and deliver results. This all leads to the final benefit—achieving personal success—the more others view you as a leader capable of achieving success, the more responsibility you will be given and the higher up in your career you will go.

The importance and benefits of being an enthusiastic leader are clear. The final question really is: how can you be more enthusiastic?

How to be More Enthusiastic

Being enthusiastic doesn't mean being outgoing, talkative, and bubbly all of the time. We will all have moments where this will be extremely difficult. However, we can all be more enthusiastic *more* of the time.

Find your purpose. If you love what you do, it won't feel like work. You'll be motivated to keep moving forward and passionate about what you're actually doing. It's hard to sustain the energy or drive for something you don't love. Based on your circumstances, it may be hard to change jobs or careers. That's okay. Find something about your job today that gives you a sense of purpose and let that drive you.

Surround yourself with passionate people. While you can be passionate and enthusiastic by yourself, it's much easier to stay positive and motivated when you're surrounded by passionate people. We can't always choose our coworkers. We have to work with people who may be less energetic, or downright negative, in order to be successful. But when you have the ability to choose members of your team, think about how passionate they are and whether they would be inspiring to the team and to yourself. In addition, outside of work, surround yourself with people who are ambitious and motivated to be the best version of themselves.

Age is Just a Number

It was early in the morning. The boat was rocking, and it was already hot. Each week, all of our unit directors and managers met up for a physical training session. It was a chance to build camaraderie and work out in the fresh air. There were eleven of us on the flight deck of the old Navy ship, myself included, huffing and puffing in our assigned groups. There was one group of two that was outperforming the others in every exercise. They were louder, faster, more energetic, and were encouraging everyone else without missing an exercise.

Watching this group of two run around, jump, do push-ups, and perform every other exercise I was throwing at them, no one would have thought they were over forty. In general, enthusiasm, especially when associated with rigorous physical activity, tends to decline with age in the military. With the exception of myself, those two were at least ten years older than everyone else. But, the intensity with which they moved was motivating the other groups to try and keep up. No one wanted to be outdone or outperformed by these two, widely considered the "older generation" in our unit. More than that, though, the genuine enjoyment on their faces made the session tolerable for everyone. No one wanted to be up early, in the heat, running around and doing all sorts of calisthenic exercises. But everyone was doing it without any complaint, and that was largely due to the motivation coming from this group of two.

Lap after lap, burpee after burpee, I saw the other groups periodically look over at the group of two just grinding out their exercises. Then the groups would pick up their pace in an effort to try and keep up. The group of two was the first to finish all the laps and exercises. Instead of getting out of the heat and showering, they stayed until everyone finished. Like true leaders, they continued to run with each group, providing encouragement every step of the way. When there was only one group left, I looked around, and all eleven directors and managers were still present. Everyone was now running with the last group, encouraging them to finish strong. The group of two had inspired and motivated the other Marines by just being themselves and finding the joy in the moment.

Recharge your battery. When things are going well, it's easy to be positive. But, when something pushes us off course, it can be easy to sink into a negative spiral of thoughts. The key is to catch yourself. When this happens, call someone who is passionate and enthusiastic. Don't dump your negativity onto them. Instead, talk about your lives, what ups and downs you may be going through, and ask for advice. It's okay to not be enthusiastic all of the time. The problem is not being enthusiastic at all.

Be authentic. We've said this before, and it rings true for enthusiasm too. Do not fake enthusiasm. People can see right through it. If you're not an overly enthusiastic person by nature, just give in to enthusiasm on an upcoming project or work task. Then observe how your enthusiastic response was contagious.

Communicate. If you're so focused on your own work all day, how can you inspire enthusiasm and passion in others? You can't. In this time of COVID-19 and remote work, speak up in team meetings and talk about your excitement for an upcoming project or even an upcoming personal endeavor. Leaders communicate their vision and recognize others.

Embrace bad news. The quickest way to become derailed and spiral into negativity is by focusing on bad news or setbacks. Instead, understand that bad news is a challenge to overcome on your way to your ultimate goal. In a few years, when you look back on the bad news, you may even be grateful for a particular setback because of what you learned along the way.

Have you ever been in a meeting and that one person walks in, and it feels like they've completely sucked the air out of the room? The energy level plummets. The laughing stops, and everyone can't wait to get out of the meeting as fast as possible? That feeling you experienced is the reason why enthusiasm in leadership is necessary. No one wanted to follow that leader. No one wanted to be around that leader. While it may not be second nature for you to be enthusiastic and upbeat all of the time, try incorporating some of the items above into your everyday routine. Make enthusiasm a habit and it will become easier. But, be careful of its dark side.

The Dark Side of Enthusiasm

What can go wrong when you're positive and motivated? Passion is inspirational after all. However, too much passion and enthusiasm can have unintended consequences. Every organization has unspoken rules and expectations that make up their organizational culture. Think of these like the rules of engagement or the social norms for a particular company. What may be seen as a "go-getter" attitude in a technology start-up could be seen as "toe-stepping" or "eager beaver" behavior in a financial services company. Showing too much passion can backfire in these instances and hurt your reputation or brand. While you shouldn't change who you are, if you are naturally a very enthusiastic person, you should consider your environment.

Additionally, when a leader is overly enthusiastic, it can come across as if they have rose colored glasses on. Just like with courage, it's important to face reality and not hide behind false positivity. Yes, you can be positive and remain energized in the face of setbacks, but don't let your enthusiasm cloud what needs to get done. As a leader, you need to be prepared for obstacles, especially if the goal is a difficult one. Find the balance between being enthusiastic and being real.

Putting It into Practice

Enthusiasm is an interesting leadership trait because it can be difficult to *teach* in the traditional sense. It's more of a mindset that others emulate. Simply being around someone who is energized and motivated is contagious. Below are a few things you can start doing today to help you become more enthusiastic.

Create a "why" statement. Simon Sinek is famous for popularizing the need to always start with your "why" statement. A "why" statement helps communicate your purpose. It serves as an anchor in decision-making, and it keeps you motivated. Maintaining motivation is about the vision. What are you trying to achieve? Your "why" statement is all about why you do what you do. What drives you and inspires you. A "why" statement should be simple, clear, actionable, use positive language, and focus on how you will further others or help them. We each have "why" statements, and they are part of our business profiles and are clearly displayed on LinkedIn. These statements keep us focused on what matters and what our purpose is. When we stay true to our "why" statements, we are excited and energized about the work we're doing.

Reread or write your goals. What are your goals? Where do you want to be three years from now? How about in ten years? What are you working towards? If you don't have any personal or professional goals written down, now is the time. Some people put vision boards together of things they want to do or places they want to see or where they see their lives in the future. This visual reminder serves as their motivation to keep going and to reach those goals. You don't need magazines and glue to create a visual reminder. Just write your goals down. Separate them into two categories: professional and personal. On the professional side, think about your career. Where would you like to see your career in the coming years? Do you have a specific job title in mind that you would like to achieve? Would you like to start your own business? Whatever your goals, write them down! Do the same thing on the personal side. Then revisit these goals every quarter or after a major milestone. Be sure they still reflect what is meaningful to you.

Take a break. Right around 2:30 or 3:00 p.m. every day, we start to hit the afternoon slump. Our motivation starts to decrease. Our energy levels are sinking, and we're not focusing as well as we did in the morning. For some people, the morning time is like this. Whatever time of day it happens, it happens to all of us. Taking a break is a great way to re-energize and come back focused. This break doesn't need to be anything fancy. You can stretch, meditate, take a short walk, or even nap if you work remotely. The point is to step away for a few minutes. Check in with your energy levels throughout the day and schedule a couple of ten minute breaks on your calendar. Block that time out for you.

We all want to be around people who are genuinely upbeat, positive, and enthusiastic. They make us want to perform better and achieve our goals. They also make us smile and feel good. Tap into your energy tank to help motivate and inspire those around you.

CHAPTER 15

PUTTING IT INTO PRACTICE

For nearly twenty-three years, I ate, lived, and breathed the Marine Corps and the 14 leadership traits. Each day doing my best to honor the Marines that came before me, making my Marines and myself better. I had traveled the world, fought in wars, and observed some of the brightest military leaders around the globe. I also had the privilege of working in two US. Embassies, hand in hand with some of the most compassionate and dedicated men and women I have ever met. It was in those experiences that I learned about and developed my own leadership style. Regardless of the position or rank of the person that I observed or interacted with, I found leadership takeaways. Even in negative situations, there were learning moments that I would add to my leadership toolbox—mainly things not to do or say. Don't get me wrong, I also made more than my fair share of mistakes and had to apologize or make amends. But I learned from each and every one of them.

Throughout my career, I was relentless and passionate about making my Marines the best versions of themselves. It was sometimes this passion for the job that could be misconstrued as a loss of bearing and tact. From curse-laden, fiery speeches before a big training operation to "you're better than this" rants. Each came from a good place yet could have been better executed on my part.

Truth be told, I know now having worked in the business world for a couple of years, those losses of bearing and tact would not be tolerated outside of the Marine Corps. In order to be successful in the business world in any facet, I've had to adapt my leadership style and approach to be more tactful, approachable, and flexible. I often utilized the leadership traits I learned in the Marine Corps while in uniform, but in the business world, I rely on them so much more.

Just like my leadership journey, missteps and all, you're on your own journey. If you've made it this far, congratulations! You've definitely taken the first step in understanding leadership traits and have most likely thought about your own leadership style and traits along the way.

As we've described, leadership traits drive behaviors, and behaviors drive success. These traits help define the type of leader you are as well as the type of leader you aspire to be. Leadership traits aren't just a list of adjectives or verbs. They are not meant to be all-encompassing and exhaustive. These traits are meant to define who you are as a leader and what you find most important. As you've seen with the Marine Corps traits, all are interconnected and intertwined. For example, good judgment leads to decisiveness and good decision-making. Or integrity leads to justice and loyalty.

There are thousands of articles and books available which talk about "the most important" leadership traits or skills. Some of these traits are universal and included on each of these lists, while others greatly differ depending on the source. What we've provided to you are the fourteen leadership traits of the US Marine Corps. There may be traits here that resonate with you and others which you don't find important to your own leadership brand, whether on an individual level or at an organizational level. That's okay.

In this chapter, we are going to walk you through the process of defining your own leadership traits and how you can put these traits into practice immediately. This process can be used at an individual level to define your own leadership traits or at an organizational level, to help define the leadership traits that are most important to your company.

Starting Point

Before we dive into defining your leadership traits, let's talk about where you are today and where you see yourself in the future.

Ask yourself these questions:

What inspires me to be a leader? First and foremost, think about why you want to be a leader. Being a leader isn't about a title or a particular level in your organization. You can be the CEO and still not be a leader. Hema has worked for that type of CEO in the past. Leadership is about your actions and behaviors. Try to make this one sentence that serves as your purpose for being a leader. This is similar to Simon Sinek's "why" statement we previously talked about.

How does it feel to be led by me? If you manage others, this is a question you will want to ask them. We all have our own view of our leadership. The true lens is how others feel when you are their leader. Ask three to four people and listen to their responses. If you don't currently manage people, consider asking instead, "How does it feel to work with me?" These questions may catch people off guard. Just explain that you are working on personal development and developing your leadership traits and their input and feedback is valuable in that process.

Who is impacted by the decisions I make and the work I do in my current role? Think about each of your stakeholders (team members, customers, investors, vendors, etc.). Also consider how each of your stakeholders is impacted by those decisions and actions.

What traits do people currently associate with me? This is where soliciting feedback is always important as well. Think about this in terms of, "What am I currently known for?" Pay attention to the words that others use when providing you with feedback. For example, after a presentation, if a coworker says, "You were really engaging. I just wish the PowerPoint was better," what did you hear? Clearly, they think you have strong speaking and communication skills. But, did you focus on the technical skill mentioned? Remember feedback is always provided through another person's lens. As a leader, that lens is important because it's how someone else views you.

Am I consistent in my behaviors and decisions? As we've talked about, leadership is about consistency and treating others equitably and fairly. Think about whether your mood or the level of person you are interacting with affects how you behave.

Where am I an expert or an emerging expert? This is about defining your core technical strengths and then thinking about how they play into your future. Think about the areas you know better than others. Maybe you're great at brand development and want to lead a marketing team one day. Or you're in sales with the dream of leading your own sales organization in the future.

What does success look like? Think about this question in terms of your current position as well as future position. Remember that what is required of you at each level may differ. For example, today you may be required to research an answer and present options. In the future, you may be required to analyze those solutions and make a decision.

As a leader, what do I want to be known for? Start by making a list of your strengths. If you're not sure what your strengths are, you can ask others. There are also assessments you can take, like Clifton Strengths, formerly known as StrengthsFinder, to help you determine your strengths. These strengths should be adjectives. For Hema, words like *Futuristic, Strategic,* and *Adaptable* come to mind. For Mike, words like *Achiever, Consistent,* and *Responsible* come to mind.

Be honest as you answer the questions above. Honesty is essential as you build or further your brand and reputation as a leader. While these questions are targeted at individuals, the questions can also help organizations determine the starting point for their leaders.

Defining Your Leadership Traits

Once you know where you are today, where you want to be in the future, and what type of leader you aspire to be, you can start thinking about your leadership traits. Before we do that, let's review the 14 leadership traits of the US Marine Corps:

> 1. *Judgment*: The ability to weigh facts and possible courses of action in order to make sound decisions.

2. *Justice*: Giving reward and punishment according to the merits of the case in question. The ability to administer a system of rewards and punishments impartially and consistently.

3. *Dependability*: The certainty of proper performance of duty.

4. *Integrity*: Uprightness of character and soundness of moral principles. The quality of truthfulness and honesty.

5. *Decisiveness*: The ability to make decisions promptly and to announce them in a clear, forceful manner.

6. *Tact*: The ability to deal with others in a manner that will maintain good relations and avoid offense. More simply stated, tact is the ability to say and do the right thing at the right time.

7. *Initiative*: Taking action in the absence of orders.

8. *Endurance*: The mental and physical stamina measured by the ability to withstand pain, fatigue, stress, and hardship.

9. *Bearing*: Creating a favorable impression in carriage, appearance, and personal conduct at all times.

10. *Unselfishness*: Avoidance of providing for one's own comfort and personal advancement at the expense of others.

11. *Courage*: Courage is a mental quality that recognizes fear of danger or criticism but enables a Marine to proceed in the face of danger with calmness and firmness.

12. *Knowledge*: Understanding of a science or an art. The range of one's information, including professional knowledge and understanding of your Marines.

13. *Loyalty*: The quality of faithfulness to country, Corps, unit, seniors, subordinates and peers.

14. *Enthusiasm*: Motivation is contagious.

As you read through these traits, which ones stood out for you? Pick your top three to five and write them down. Why did these traits stand out?

In looking at your list, are there any that are missing? If so, write those down as well. The list should have around eight to ten leadership traits that you feel connected to.

Next, rank order all of the traits, with one being the most important leadership trait to you.

Look at this list. How does it feel to you? Are these the traits of a leader you would like to follow? Keep refining the list until you feel aligned with the traits and the answer to the second question is a resounding yes. Try to get the list down to about four to six traits that are meaningful and impactful for you. Next, define each of these traits. Get a solid and clear understanding of what each one means and how it relates to you, whether now or in the future.

Writing a Leadership Statement

Organizations have Mission, Vision, and Value statements (MVV for short). Your organization most likely has these as well. A leadership statement serves as an individual MVV. This statement outlines your leadership purpose, vision and values, taking into account those traits you identified above.

The statement needs to be true to you, your behaviors, and motivations as a leader and it must be something you can follow every day. A leadership statement can be multiple sentences. For example, "I am a reliable, focused, decisive, and charismatic leader. I am known for being a high performer and creating high-performing teams that inspire others to bring their best effort every day and to reach peak performance. I remain calm under pressure and maintain my bearing at all times. When I do well, my team does well."

Leadership statements can also be one sentence. For example, "I am known for being decisive, dependable, courageous and unselfish so that I can lead with integrity and enthusiasm."

Whether short or long, it's important the statement resonates with you and that you use it to motivate yourself daily as a leader. Pressure test your statement. Explain to confidants, coworkers, and your manager that you are on a journey to define your leadership traits and that you've put together a leadership statement. This is deeper than just getting feedback. It's about holding yourself accountable to your statement. The more you socialize and display it, the better the chances it will become part of your every day.

Print the statement out and display it at your desk or in your office. In Malcolm Gladwell's book *Outliers*, he discusses why it takes 10,000 hours of practice to become an expert in anything. Leadership is the same way. Consider your leadership statement not only your mantra but what you need to practice.

Defining Your Leadership Principles

Leadership principles are actions or guiding beliefs that leaders use to achieve success. These principles are based on the leadership traits and guide behavior.

The Marine Corps has 11 Leadership Principles:

1. Know yourself and seek self-improvement.
2. Be technically and tactically proficient.
3. Know your Marines and look out for their welfare.
4. Keep your Marines informed.
5. Set the example.

6. Ensure the task is understood, supervised, and accomplished.

7. Train your Marines as a team.

8. Make sound and timely decisions.

9. Develop a sense of responsibility among your subordinates.

10. Employ your command in accordance with its capabilities.

11. Seek responsibility and take responsibility for your actions.

As you read through these, did you notice the leadership traits that are embedded in these actions? For example, *Knowledge* is represented in principle 2. *Decisiveness* in principle 8. In some of the others, we see *Integrity, Unselfishness,* and *Courage.* These principles all start with an action word. These are things that leaders should be doing.

Take a look at your final leadership traits. How do they translate to a leadership principle? What is the specific action? A couple of examples are, "Be human and admit mistakes," or "Work together to achieve greater success," or "Be curious and continuously learn new things." These principles shouldn't be too generic. Things like, "Lead by example" or "Leadership is about people" are meaningless. Of course you should lead by example and of course leadership is about people. But, so what? How do they relate to *your* leadership traits?

We're not going to spend a lot of time on leadership principles other than to say they help drive your leadership traits throughout all of your interactions. The first step is really developing the traits and your leadership statement. Think about leadership principles as the next step in your leadership journey.

The Evolution of Your Leadership

As we've said a few times, leadership is a journey. Where you are today as a leader, regardless of how long you've been a leader, will be different from where you will be as a leader one year, three years, or even five years from now. This also means your leadership traits can evolve as well. What is important to you today may not be as meaningful for you as a leader a few years from now. While we said to have four to six leadership traits, chances are you may have three to four additional ones, which are further down on your list. These traits may move up as time goes on.

Revisit your leadership traits every so often, especially if your role changes. Same applies to your leadership statement. Be fluid and understand your statement should grow as you grow. It may evolve depending on what is required of you as a leader in any given position. The critical piece is to ensure your traits and statement are representative of who you are as a leader and what your values are.

Now that you have your leadership traits, leadership statement, and a few leadership principles, it's time to move on to your commitments. What are you going to do to ensure you follow your leadership statement? Write down three to five tangible commitments that you can easily measure to ensure you are set up for success in following your leadership strategy. For example, if one of your leadership traits is *unselfishness*, a commitment could be, "Check in with the team once per week to determine how decisions affect everyone versus just myself." Another example is, "Meet once a quarter with a cross-functional leader to learn more about the implications of my team's work." This can speak to *inclusivity*.

Lastly, there are many tools available to help you along this leadership journey. This can include formal training, mentoring, coaching, self-training through books (like this one!), and articles. You can also solicit feedback from others and do some serious introspection, especially if you find yourself straying from your leadership traits and leadership statement. Tap into your resources. Doing so isn't a sign of weakness, but a sign of courage, and also shows how important being a strong leader is to you.

Above all else, don't forget to intentionally pause and breathe. Leadership is a tough yet deeply meaningful and impactful job. In the words of John Donahoe, CEO of Nike, "Leadership is a journey, not a destination. It is a process and not an outcome."

You are clearly already on the leadership journey. Keep moving forward and be proud of the progress you've already made!

BONUS

If you would like to continue the leadership discussion, follow us on social media and connect with us on LinkedIn.

For downloadable resources, as well as a guide on how to create your own leadership traits, check out our website at www.cultureandleadershipbooks. com.

ABOUT THE AUTHORS

 **Hema Crockett** is an award-winning business leader, entrepreneur and former HR executive, who led successful teams in the private sector as well as internationally for the US State Department and the Department of Justice. She is the co-founder of the advisory firm High Performanceology and also modern talent agency Gig Talent and utilizes her expertise to create environments where employees can thrive and grow. Hema is a certified executive coach, and a highly sought-after speaker on a range of topics in entrepreneurship, individual and team leadership and organizational culture. She has been published in *Forbes* and *Thrive Global*, among other publications. Hema is also co-author of *Designing Exceptional Organizational Cultures: How to Develop Companies Where Employees Thrive.*

 **Michael Crockett** (USMC, Ret.) served the US military for twenty-three years, in combat as a member of the legendary "fighting" Fifth Marines and as leader at the School of Infantry. An expert in the Marines' Fourteen Leadership Traits, he oversaw units at Seal Beach and Air Station Miramar, and was the Senior Marine Corps Official at the US Embassies in Kathmandu and Berlin. Michael earned his B.A. in Organizational Management from Ashford University and is now the head of Business Operations and Leadership Development for High Performanceology and Gig Talent, alongside his wife, Hema.

Both Hema and Michael live in San Diego.